AS I WALKED OUT ONE EVENING

also by W. H. Auden

Collected Poems
Selected Poems
Collected Shorter Poems
Collected Longer Poems
The English Auden:
Poems, Essays & Dramatic Writings
Auden's Juvenilia
Paul Bunyan
A Certain World:
A Commonplace Book
The Enchafèd Flood
Secondary Worlds
The Dyer's Hand

with Christopher Isherwood
Plays and Other Dramatic Writings
by W. H. Auden 1928–1938
The Dog Beneath the Skin
The Ascent of F6
and On the Frontier
Journey to a War

with Chester Kallman
Libretti and Other Dramatic Writings
by W. H. Auden 1939–1973

with Louis MacNeice
Letters from Iceland

with Paul Taylor
Norse Poems

with Leif Sjöberg
Markings by Dag Hammarskjöld

with Louis Kronenberger
The Faber Book of Aphorisms

by Alan Ansen
The Table Talk of W. H. Auden

As I Walked Out One Evening

Songs, ballads, lullabies,
limericks and other light verse
by **W. H. AUDEN**

Selected by Edward Mendelson

faber and faber

This collection first published in 1995
by Faber and Faber Limited
3 Queen Square London WC1N 3AU
This paperback edition first published in 1996

Phototypeset by Wilmaset Ltd, Birkenhead, Wirral
Printed in England by Clays Ltd, St Ives plc

A CIP record for this book
is available from the British Library

ISBN 0-571-17898-7

2 4 6 8 10 9 7 5 3 1

CONTENTS

Preface, ix

It's No Use Raising a Shout, 3
What's in Your Mind, My Dove, My Coney, 4
Prothalamion, 4
Alma Mater, 6
The Airman's Alphabet, 8
The Three Companions, 11
Shorts, 11
Song: 'You were a great Cunarder, I', 15
Ballad: 'O what is that sound which so thrills the ear', 15
The Witnesses, 17
Song: 'Seen when night was silent', 22
Who's Who, 23
Now Through Night's Caressing Grip, 23
In the Square, 24
Madrigal, 25
Night Mail, 26
Song: 'Let the florid music praise', 28
Foxtrot from a Play, 28
Underneath the Abject Willow, 30
Fish in the Unruffled Lakes, 31
Song: 'The chimney sweepers', 32
At Last the Secret Is Out, 32
Funeral Blues, 33
Jam Tart, 34
Death's Echo, 35
Lullaby: 'Lay your sleeping head, my love', 37
Danse Macabre, 38
Blues: 'Ladies and gentlemen, sitting here', 41
Give Up Love, 42
Nonsense Song, 44
Johnny, 44
Miss Gee, 45

Victor, 49

James Honeyman, 53

Roman Wall Blues, 58

As I Walked Out One Evening, 59

O Tell Me the Truth About Love, 61

Gare du Midi, 63

Epitaph on a Tyrant, 63

The Unknown Citizen, 64

Refugee Blues, 65

Ode, 67

Calypso, 68

Heavy Date, 69

Song: 'Warm are the still and lucky miles', 74

'Gold in the North' Came the Blizzard to Say, 75

The Glamour Boys and Girls Have Grievances Too, 76

Carry Her Over the Water, 78

Eyes Look into the Well, 78

Lady Weeping at the Crossroads, 79

Notes, 80

The Way, 85

Song for St Cecilia's Day, 85

Many Happy Returns, 88

Shepherd's Carol, 92

Song of the Old Soldier, 93

Song of the Master and Boatswain, 94

Adrian and Francisco's Song, 95

Miranda's Song, 96

Three Songs from *The Age of Anxiety*, 96

Under Which Lyre, 98

Nursery Rhyme, 104

Barcarolle, 104

Music Ho, 105

The Love Feast, 106

Song: 'Deftly, admiral, cast your fly', 107

Limericks, 108

Hunting Season, 110

The Willow-Wren and the Stare, 110
The Proof, 112
'The Truest Poetry Is the Most Feigning', 113
Nocturne, 115
Metalogue to *The Magic Flute*, 116
A Toast, 120
Some Thirty Inches from My Nose, 122
On the Circuit, 122
Song of the Ogres, 124
Song of the Devil, 125
The Geography of the House, 127
Moralities, 129
A New Year Greeting, 137
Doggerel by a Senior Citizen, 139

Notes, 143

Index of Titles and First Lines, 149

This book is a selection of Auden's most immediately accessible poems. These poems, which include some of his greatest work, have all the profundity and complexity of his more difficult poems, but they also have the direct emotional and rhythmic appeal of traditional ballads, popular songs, rhyming games for children, and rude limericks for adults. In writing each of these poems, Auden challenged himself to transform a conventional form or familiar style into a fresh source of wisdom, surprise, and delight. And he chose to write many of his poems in accessible styles because they allowed him to write about emotion and experience that more difficult and obscure styles would falsify or distort.

Unlike many of his contemporary poets, Auden did not write in one manner for an élite learned audience and another style for a larger popular audience. In fact, he did not write for any collective or general audiences at all. He wrote for each of his individual readers, and for all the variations and moods in each reader's life. He knew that a reader who in one mood prefers tragedy will want farce in another, and he knew that the most serious moods do not necessarily call for the most solemn poems:

> Even a limerick
>   ought to be something a man of
> honour, awaiting death from cancer or a firing-squad,
>   could read without contempt: (at
> *that* frontier I wouldn't dare speak to anyone
>   in either a prophet's bellow
> or a diplomat's whisper.)

He wrote these lines late in his life, in 'The Cave of Making', an elegy for his fellow poet Louis MacNeice. Three decades earlier, in 'Letter to Lord Byron', he had written in a similar vein:

Only on varied diet can we live.
The pious fable and the dirty story
Share in the total literary glory.

Auden's first published book, *Poems*, appeared in 1930, when he was twenty-three. His friend Naomi Mitchison complained in a review that some of the poems were overly obscure. 'Am I really so obscure?' he asked her in a letter. 'Obscurity is a bad fault.' He was then emerging from a phase in which he had tried to outdo the early T. S. Eliot in writing poems made up of fragments and allusions, and he had begun to write verse that he hoped would be as suitable for the cabaret and theatre as for the printed page.

From 1932 until 1938 he wrote musical plays for the experimental and often chaotic productions of the Group Theatre. The Group was the creation of the dancer Rupert Doone and the painter Robert Medley; it had been Medley who started Auden on his career as a poet by casually asking him at school if he had ever written any poems. Auden wrote almost all his work for the Group in collaboration – his plays were written jointly with Christopher Isherwood, with lyrics written to be set by Benjamin Britten – and the shared act of collaboration helped him escape the solitary obscurities of his earliest poems. At the same time, he found that he could write most easily about his emotional life in songs for the soprano voice of Hedli Anderson (whom he met when she performed with the Group Theatre). Behind the mask of Hedli Anderson he could tell truths that would sound egocentric and false if he spoke of them in his own person.

For a few years after he settled in America in 1939 he continued to write song lyrics, some of them in calypso and wild-west accents that he had not heard in England. But during the 1940s and 1950s his songs became more contemplative and infrequent, and instead of musical plays he wrote opera libretti in collaboration with Chester Kallman.

In the 1960s, however, he again began writing lighter poems for public performance. The initial impulse was a commission to write the lyrics for the musical comedy *Man of La Mancha*, although the producer found Auden's contributions too thoughtful and replaced him with a lyricist more palatable for Broadway. Also in the 1960s, his agent began to arrange annual reading tours for him at American colleges and universities, and many of his later poems were written to unsettle and delight the listeners who, with a generosity that always amazed him, paid to hear him read. He also read to poetry festivals and other audiences in America and Europe, and died a few hours after his last public reading, in Vienna in 1973.

The poems in this book have been chosen according to the principles that Auden specified in his introduction to *The Oxford Book of Light Verse*, an anthology that he compiled in 1937:

> When the things in which the poet is interested, the things which he sees about him, are much the same as those of his audience, and that audience is a fairly general one, he will not be conscious of himself as an unusual person, and his language will be straightforward and close to ordinary speech. When, on the other hand, his interests and perceptions are not readily acceptable to society, or his audience is a highly specialized one, perhaps of fellow poets, he will be acutely aware of himself as the poet, and his method of expression may depart very widely from the normal social language.

> In the first case his poetry will be 'light' in the sense in which it is used in this anthology. Three kinds of poetry have been included:
> (1) Poetry written for performance, to be spoken or sung before an audience (e.g. Folk-songs, the poems of Tom Moore).

(2) Poetry intended to be read, but having for its subject-matter the everyday social life of its period or the experiences of the poet as an ordinary human being (e.g. the poems of Chaucer, Pope, Byron).

(3) Such nonsense poetry as, through its properties and techniques, has a general appeal (Nursery rhymes, the poems of Edward Lear).

Auden recognized this kind of poetry as a distinct category in his own work. He used the title 'Lighter Poems' for one of the sections of *Another Time*, a book of poems that he published in 1940. In the collected edition of his work that he published in 1945, he gathered many of his lighter poems under the heading 'Songs and Other Musical Pieces'; in a collected edition published in 1966 he gathered them in groups titled 'Ten Songs', 'Twelve Songs', and similar headings.

The arrangement of this book is chronological. A few poems are included that Auden never published or that he published in magazines but never collected in book form.

Edward Mendelson

AS I WALKED OUT ONE EVENING

It's No Use Raising a Shout

It's no use raising a shout.
No, Honey, you can cut that right out.
I don't want any more hugs;
Make me some fresh tea, fetch me some rugs.
Here am I, here are you:
But what does it mean? What are we going to do?

A long time ago I told my mother
I was leaving home to find another:
I never answered her letter
But I never found a better.
Here am I, here are you:
But what does it mean? What are we going to do?

It wasn't always like this?
Perhaps it wasn't, but it is.
Put the car away; when life fails,
What's the good of going to Wales?
Here am I, here are you:
But what does it mean? What are we going to do?

In my spine there was a base,
And I knew the general's face:
But they've severed all the wires,
And I can't tell what the general desires.
Here am I, here are you:
But what does it mean? What are we going to do?

In my veins there is a wish,
And a memory of fish:
When I lie crying on the floor,
It says, 'You've often done this before.'
Here am I, here are you:
But what does it mean? What are we going to do?

A bird used to visit this shore:
It isn't going to come any more.
I've come a very long way to prove
No land, no water, and no love.
Here am I, here are you:
But what does it mean? What are we going to do?

What's in Your Mind, My Dove, My Coney

What's in your mind, my dove, my coney;
Do thoughts grow like feathers, the dead end of life;
Is it making of love or counting of money,
Or raid on the jewels, the plans of a thief?

Open your eyes, my dearest dallier;
Let hunt with your hands for escaping me;
Go through the motions of exploring the familiar;
Stand on the brink of the warm white day.

Rise with the wind, my great big serpent;
Silence the birds and darken the air;
Change me with terror, alive in a moment;
Strike for the heart and have me there.

Prothalamion

You who return tonight to a narrow bed
With one name running sorrowfully through your
	sorrowful head,
You who have never been touched, and you, pale lover,
Who left the house this morning kissed all over,
You little boys also of quite fourteen
Beginning to realize just what we mean,
Fill up glasses with champagne and drink again.

It's not a new school or factory to which we summon,
We're here today because of a man and a woman.
O Chef, employ your continental arts
To celebrate the union of two loving hearts.
Waiters, be deft, and slip, you pages, by
To honour the god to name whom is to lie:
Fill up glasses with champagne and drink again.

Already he has brought the swallows past the Scillies
To chase each other skimming under English bridges,
Has loosed the urgent pollen on the glittering country
To find the pistil, force its burglar's entry,
He moves us also and up the marble stair
He leads the figures matched in beauty and desire:
Fill up glasses with champagne and drink again.

It's not only this we praise, it's the general love:
Let cat's mew rise to a scream on the tool-shed roof,
Let son come home tonight to his anxious mother,
Let the vicar lead the choirboy into a dark corner.
The orchid shall flower tonight that flowers every
        hundred years,
The boots and the slavey be found dutch-kissing on the
        stairs:
Fill up glasses with champagne and drink again.

Let this be kept as a generous hour by all,
This once let the uncle settle his nephew's bill,
Let the nervous lady's table gaucheness be forgiven,
Let the thief's explanation of the theft be taken,
The boy caught smoking shall escape the usual
        whipping,
Tonight the expensive whore shall give herself for
        nothing:
Fill up glasses with champagne and drink again.

The landlocked state shall get its port today,
The midnight worker in the laboratory by the sea
Shall discover under the cross-wires that which he looks
    for,
Tonight the asthmatic clerk shall dream he's a boxer,
Let the cold heart's wish be granted, the desire for a
    desire,
O give to the coward now his hour of power:
Fill up glasses with champagne and drink again.

Alma Mater

Chorus   Hail the strange electric writing
                  Alma Mater on the door
                  Like a secret sign inviting
                  All the rich to meet the poor:
                  Alma Mater, ave, salve,
                  Floreas in secula.

Girls   You sent us men with lots of money,
                  You sent us men you knew were clean,
                  You sent us men as sweet as honey,
                  Men to make us really keen.
                  Always, even though we marry,
                  Though we wear ancestral pearls,
                  One memory we'll always carry,
                  We were Alma Mater girls.

Chorus   Alma Mater, ave, salve, *etc*.

Thieves   Let Americans with purses
                  Go for short strolls after dark,
                  Let the absent-minded nurses
                  Leave an heiress in the park,
                  Though the bullers soon or later

	Clap us handcuffed into jail,
	We'll remember Alma Mater,
	We'll remember without fail.

Chorus   Alma Mater, ave, salve, *etc.*

Boys   The French are mean and Germans lazy,
Dutchmen leave you in the end.
Only the English, though they're crazy,
They will keep you for a friend.
Always, though a king in cotton
Waft us hence to foreign parts,
Alma Mater shall not be forgotten,
She is written on our hearts.

Chorus   Alma Mater, ave, salve, *etc.*

Blackmailers   We must thank our mugs' relations,
For our income and man's laws.
But the first congratulations,
Alma Mater, they are yours.

Coiners   When the fool believes our story,
When he thinks our coins are true,
To Alma Mater be the glory
For she taught us what to do.

Chorus   Alma Mater, ave, salve, *etc.*

Old Hacks   We cannot dance upon the table
and Trots   Now we're old as souvenirs
Yet as long as we are able
We'll remember bygone years.
Still, as when we were the attraction,
Come the people from abroad,
Spending, though we're out of action,
More than they can well afford.

Chorus   Alma Mater, ave, salve, *etc.*

Grand Chorus	Navies rust and nations perish,
	Currency is never sure,
	But Alma Mater she shall flourish
	While the sexes shall endure:
	Alma Mater, ave, salve,
	Floreas in secula.

The Airman's Alphabet

ACE –
Pride of parents
and photographed person
and laughter in leather.

BOMB –
Curse from cloud
and coming to crook
and saddest to steeple.

COCKPIT –
Soft seat
and support of soldier
and hold for hero.

DEATH –
Award for wildness
and worst in the west
and painful to pilots.

ENGINE –
Darling of designers
and dirty dragon
and revolving roarer.

FLYING –
Habit of hawks
and unholy hunting
and ghostly journey.

GAUGE –
Informer about oil
and important to eye
and graduated glass.

HANGAR –	Mansion of machine and motherly to metal and house of handshaking.
INSTRUMENT –	Dial on dashboard and destroyer of doubt and father of fact.
JOYSTICK –	Pivot of power and responder to pressure and grip for the glove.
KISS –	Touch taking off and tenderness in time and firmness on flesh.
LOOPING –	Flying folly and feat at fairs and brave to boys.
MECHANIC –	Owner of overalls and interested in iron and trusted with tools.
NOSE-DIVE –	Nightmare to nerves and needed by no one and dash toward death.
OBSERVER –	Peeper through periscope and peerer at pasture and eye in the air.
PROPELLER –	Wooden wind-oar and twisted whirler and lifter of load.
QUIET –	Absent from airmen and easy to horses and got in the grave.

RUDDER –   Deflector of flight
               and flexible fin
               and pointer of path.

STORM –   Night from the north
               and numbness nearing
               and hail ahead.

TIME –   Expression of alarm
               and used by the ill
               and personal space.

UNDERCARRIAGE – Softener of shock
               and seat on the soil
               and easy to injure.

VICTIM –   Corpse after crash
               and carried through country
               and atonement for aircraft.

WIRELESS –   Sender of signal
               and speaker of sorrow
               and news from nowhere.

X –   Mark upon map
               and meaning mischief
               and lovers' lingo.

YOUTH –   Daydream of devils
               and dear to the damned
               and always to us.

ZERO –   Love before leaving
               and touch of terror
               and time of attack.

The Three Companions

'O where are you going?' said reader to rider,
'That valley is fatal where furnaces burn,
Yonder's the midden whose odours will madden,
That gap is the grave where the tall return.'

'O do you imagine,' said fearer to farer,
'That dusk will delay on your path to the pass,
Your diligent looking discover the lacking
Your footsteps feel from granite to grass?'

'O what was that bird', said horror to hearer,
'Did you see that shape in the twisted trees?
Behind you swiftly the figure comes softly,
The spot on your skin is a shocking disease?'

'Out of this house' – said rider to reader
'Yours never will' – said farer to fearer
'They're looking for you' – said hearer to horror
As he left them there, as he left them there.

Shorts

Pick a quarrel, go to war
Leave the hero in the bar.
Hunt the lion, climb the peak.
No one guesses you are weak.

*

The friends of the born nurse
Are always getting worse.

*

You're a long way off from becoming a saint
As long as you suffer from any complaint:
But if you don't, there's no denying
The chances are that you're not trying.

*

Man would be happy, loving and sage
If he didn't keep lying about his age.

*

Tommy did as mother told him
    Till his soul had split:
One half thought of angels
    And the other half of shit.

*

Willy, finding half a soul,
Went abroad to find the whole.
He went by land, he went by sea
But never found it: Thomas Cook
For every effort that he took
Received the customary fee.

*

Desire for death in the morning
    Is cancer's warning.
Desire for life at night
    Is mania in sight.

*

Schoolboy, making lonely maps:
Better do it with some chaps.

*

The pleasures of the English nation:
Copotomy and Sodulation.

*

Let us honour if we can
The vertical man
Though we value none
But the horizontal one.

*

I am beginning to lose patience
With my personal relations.
They are not deep
And they are not cheap.

*

I'm afraid there's many a spectacled sod
Prefers the British Museum to God.

*

There are two kinds of friendship even in babes:
Two against one and seven against Thebes.

*

Private faces in public places
Are wiser and nicer
Than public faces in private places.

*

Come kiss me now, you old brown cow
The doctor's said you're balmy.
The maid at the vicar's has torn her knickers
I'm off to join the army.

*

Don't know my father's name,
I am my mother's shame.
I mayn't die all the same,
    I'm still too young.

*

If yer wants to see me agyne
    Then come to the stytion before the tryne.
In the general wytin' 'all
    We'll see each other fer the very las' time of all.

*

Alice is gone and I'm alone,
    Nobody understands
How lovely were her Fire Alarms,
    How fair her German Bands.

O how I cried when Alice died
    The day we were to have wed.
We never had our Roasted Duck
    And now she's a Loaf of Bread.

14

At nights I weep, I cannot sleep:
　　Moonlight to me recalls
I never saw her Waterfront
　　Nor she my Waterfalls.

Song

You were a great Cunarder, I
Was only a fishing smack.
Once you passed across my bows
And of course you did not look back.
I was only a single moment yet
I watch the sea and sigh,
Because my heart can never forget
The day you passed me by.

Ballad

O what is that sound which so thrills the ear
　　Down in the valley drumming, drumming?
Only the scarlet soldiers, dear,
　　　　The soldiers coming.

O what is that light I see flashing so clear
　　Over the distance brightly, brightly?
Only the sun on their weapons, dear,
　　　　As they step lightly.

O what are they doing with all that gear;
　　What are they doing this morning, this morning?
Only the usual manoeuvres, dear,
　　　　Or perhaps a warning.

O why have they left the road down there;
	Why are they suddenly wheeling, wheeling?
Perhaps a change in the orders, dear;
		Why are you kneeling?

O haven't they stopped for the doctor's care;
	Haven't they reined their horses, their horses?
Why, they are none of them wounded, dear,
		None of these forces.

O is it the parson they want with white hair;
	Is it the parson, is it, is it?
No, they are passing his gateway, dear,
		Without a visit.

O it must be the farmer who lives so near;
	It must be the farmer so cunning, so cunning?
They have passed the farm already, dear,
		And now they are running.

O where are you going? stay with me here!
	Were the vows you swore me deceiving, deceiving?
No, I promised to love you, dear,
		But I must be leaving.

O it's broken the lock and splintered the door,
	O it's the gate where they're turning, turning;
Their feet are heavy on the floor
		And their eyes are burning.

The Witnesses

You dowagers with Roman noses
Sailing along between banks of roses
    well dressed,
You Lords who sit at committee tables
And crack with grooms in riding stables
    your father's jest;

Solicitors with poker faces,
And doctors with black bags to cases
    hurried,
Reporters coming home at dawn
And heavy bishops on the lawn
    by sermons worried;

You stokers lit by furnace-glare,
And you, too, steeplejacks up there
    singing,
You shepherds wind-blown on the ridges,
Tramps leaning over village bridges
    your eardrums ringing;

On land, on sea, in field, in town
Attend: Musician put them down,
    those trumpets;
Let go, young lover, of her hand
Come forward both of you and stand
    as still as limpets

Close as you can and listen well:
My companion here is about to tell
    a story;
Peter, Pontius Pilate, Paul
Whoever you are, it concerns you all
    and human glory.

Call him Prince Alpha if you wish
He was born in a palace, his people were swish;
     his christening
Was called by the Tatler the event of the year,
All the photographed living were there
     and the dead were listening.

You would think I was trying to foozle you
If I told you all that kid could do;
     enough
To say he was never afraid of the dark
He climbed all the trees in his pater's park;
     his nurse thought him rough.

At school his brilliance was a mystery,
All languages, science, maths, and history
     he knew;
His style at cricket was simply stunning
At rugger, soccer, hockey, running
     and swimming too.

The days went by, he grew mature;
He was a looker you may be sure,
     so straight
Old couples cried 'God bless my soul
I thought that man was a telegraph pole'
     when he passed their gate.

His eyes were blue as a mountain lake,
He made the hearts of the girls to ache;
     he was strong;
He was gay, he was witty, his speaking voice
Sounded as if a large Rolls Royce
     had passed along.

He kissed his dear old mater one day,
He said to her 'I'm going away,
      good-bye'.
No sword nor terrier by his side
He set off through the world so wide
      under the sky.

Where did he travel? Where didn't he travel?
Over the ice and over the gravel
      and the sea;
Up the fevered jungle river,
Through haunted forests without a shiver
      he wandered free.

What did he do? What didn't he do,
He rescued maidens, overthrew
      ten giants
Like factory chimneys, slaughtered dragons,
Though their heads were larger than railway wagons
      tamed their defiance.

What happened, what happened? I'm coming to that;
He came to a desert and down he sat
      and cried,
Above the blue sky arching wide
Two tall rocks as black as pride
      on either side.

There on a stone he sat him down,
Around the desert stretching brown
      like the tide,
Above the blue sky arching wide
Two black rocks on either side
      and, O how he cried.

'I thought my strength could know no stemming
But I was foolish as a lemming;
         for what
Was I born, was it only to see
I'm as tired of life as life of me?
         let me be forgot.

'Children have heard of my every action
It gives me no sort of satisfaction
         and why?
Let me get this as clear as I possibly can
No, I am not the truly strong man,
         O let me die.'

There in the desert all alone
He sat for hours on a long flat stone
         and sighed;
Above the blue sky arching wide
Two black rocks on either side,
         and then he died.

Now ladies and gentlemen, big and small,
This story of course has a morale;
         again
Unless like him you wish to die
Listen, while my friend and I
         proceed to explain.

III

What had he done to be treated thus?
If you want to know, he'd offended us:
         for yes,
We guard the wells, we're handy with a gun,
We've a very special sense of fun,
         we curse and bless.

You are the town, and we are the clock,
We are the guardians of the gate in the rock,
          the Two;
On your left, and on your right
In the day, and in the night
          we are watching you.

Wiser not to ask just what has occurred
To them that disobeyed our word;
          to those
We were the whirlpool, we were the reef,
We were the formal nightmare, grief,
          and the unlucky rose.

Climb up the cranes, learn the sailors' words
When the ships from the islands, laden with birds
          come in;
Tell your stories of fishing and other men's wives,
The expansive moments of constricted lives,
          in the lighted inn.

By all means say of the peasant youth
'That person there is in the truth'
          we're kind,
Tire of your little rut and look it,
You have to obey but you don't have to like it,
          we do not mind:

But do not imagine we do not know
Or that what you hide with care won't show
          at a glance;
Nothing is done, nothing is said
But don't make the mistake of thinking us dead;
          I shouldn't dance

For I'm afraid in that case you'll have a fall;
We've been watching you over the garden wall
       for hours,
The sky is darkening like a stain,
Something is going to fall like rain
       and it won't be flowers.

When the green field comes off like a lid
Revealing what were much better hid,
       unpleasant;
And look! behind you without a sound
The woods have come up and are standing round
       in deadly crescent.

The bolt is sliding in its groove,
Outside the window is the black remov-
       ers' van,
And now with sudden swift emergence
Come the women in dark glasses, the hump-backed
       surgeons
       and the scissor-man.

This might happen any day
So be careful what you say
       or do
Be clean, be tidy, oil the lock,
Trim the garden, wind the clock:
       Remember the Two.

Song

      Seen when night was silent,
      The bean-shaped island

      And our ugly comic servant
      Who is observant

O the verandah and the fruit
    The tiny steamer in the bay
Startling summer with its hoot.
    You have gone away.

Who's Who

A shilling life will give you all the facts:
How Father beat him, how he ran away,
What were the struggles of his youth, what acts
Made him the greatest figure of his day:
Of how he fought, fished, hunted, worked all night,
Though giddy, climbed new mountains; named a sea:
Some of the last researchers even write
Love made him weep his pints like you and me.

With all his honours on, he sighed for one
Who, say astonished critics, lived at home;
Did little jobs about the house with skill
And nothing else; could whistle; would sit still
Or potter round the garden; answered some
Of his long marvellous letters but kept none.

Now Through Night's Caressing Grip

Now through night's caressing grip
Earth and all her oceans slip,
Capes of China slide away
From her fingers into day
And the Americas incline
Coasts towards her shadow line.
Now the ragged vagrants creep
Into crooked holes to sleep:
Just and unjust, worst and best,
Change their places as they rest:

Awkward lovers lie in fields
Where disdainful beauty yields:
While the splendid and the proud
Naked stand before the crowd
And the losing gambler gains
And the beggar entertains:
May sleep's healing power extend
Through these hours to our friend.
Unpursued by hostile force,
Traction engine, bull or horse
Or revolting succubus;
Calmly till the morning break
Let him lie, then gently wake.

In the Square

O for doors to be open and an invite with gilded edges
To dine with Lord Lobcock and Count Asthma on the
    platinum benches,
With the somersaults and fireworks, the roast and the
                smacking kisses –
            Cried the six cripples to the silent statue,
            The six beggared cripples.

And Garbo's and Cleopatra's wits to go astraying,
In a feather ocean with me to go fishing and playing
Still jolly when the cock has burst himself with crowing –
            Cried the six cripples to the silent statue,
            The six beggared cripples.

And to stand on green turf among the craning yellow
                faces,
Dependent on the chestnut, the sable, and Arabian
                horses,

And me with a magic crystal to foresee their places –
        Cried the six cripples to the silent statue,
        The six beggared cripples.

And this square to be a deck, and these pigeons sails to rig
And to follow the delicious breeze like a tantony pig
To the shaded feverless islands where the melons are big –
        Cried the six cripples to the silent statue,
        The six beggared cripples.

And these shops to be turned to tulips in a garden bed,
And me with my stick to thrash each merchant dead
As he pokes from a flower his bald and wicked head –
        Cried the six cripples to the silent statue,
        The six beggared cripples.

And a hole in the bottom of heaven, and Peter and Paul
And each smug surprised saint like parachutes to fall,
And every one-legged beggar to have no legs at all –
        Cried the six cripples to the silent statue,
        The six beggared cripples.

Madrigal

O lurcher-loving collier, black as night,
Follow your love across the smokeless hill;
Your lamp is out and all the cages still;
Course for her heart and do not miss,
For Sunday soon is past and, Kate, fly not so fast,
For Monday comes when none may kiss:
Be marble to his soot, and to his black be white.

Night Mail

(Commentary for a G.P.O. Film)

I

This is the Night Mail crossing the Border,
Bringing the cheque and the postal order,

Letters for the rich, letters for the poor,
The shop at the corner, the girl next door.

Pulling up Beattock, a steady climb:
The gradient's against her, but she's on time.

Past cotton-grass and moorland boulder,
Shovelling white steam over her shoulder,

Snorting noisily, she passes
Silent miles of wind-bent grasses.

Birds turn their heads as she approaches,
Stare from bushes at her blank-faced coaches.

Sheep-dogs cannot turn her course;
They slumber on with paws across.

In the farm she passes no one wakes,
But a jug in a bedroom gently shakes.

II

Dawn freshens. Her climb is done.
Down towards Glasgow she descends,
Towards the steam tugs yelping down a glade
      of cranes,
Towards the fields of apparatus, the furnaces
Set on the dark plain like gigantic chessmen.
All Scotland waits for her:
In dark glens, beside pale-green lochs,
Men long for news.

Letters of thanks, letters from banks,
Letters of joy from girl and boy,
Receipted bills and invitations
To inspect new stock or to visit relations,
And applications for situations,
And timid lovers' declarations,
And gossip, gossip from all the nations,
News circumstantial, news financial,
Letters with holiday snaps to enlarge in,
Letters with faces scrawled on the margin,
Letters from uncles, cousins and aunts,
Letters to Scotland from the South of France,
Letters of condolence to Highlands and Lowlands,
Written on paper of every hue,
The pink, the violet, the white and the blue,
That chatty, the catty, the boring, the adoring,
The cold and official and the heart's outpouring,
Clever, stupid, short and long,
The typed and the printed and the spelt all wrong.

IV

Thousands are still asleep,
Dreaming of terrifying monsters
Or a friendly tea beside the band in Cranston's or
　　Crawford's:
Asleep in working Glasgow, asleep in well-set
　　Edinburgh,
Asleep in granite Aberdeen,
They continue their dreams,
But shall wake soon and hope for letters,
And none will hear the postman's knock
Without a quickening of the heart.
For who can bear to feel himself forgotten?

Song

Let the florid music praise,
        The flute and the trumpet,
Beauty's conquest of your face:
In that land of flesh and bone,
Where from citadels on high
Her imperial standards fly,
        Let the hot sun
        Shine on, shine on.

O but the unloved have had power,
        The weeping and striking,
Always; time will bring their hour:
Their secretive children walk
Through your vigilance of breath
To unpardonable death,
        And my vows break
        Before his look.

Foxtrot from a Play

The soldier loves his rifle,
        The scholar loves his books,
The farmer loves his horses,
        The film star loves her looks.
There's love the whole world over
        Wherever you may be;
Some lose their rest for gay Mae West,
        But you're my cup of tea.

Some talk of Alexander
	And some of Fred Astaire,
Some like their heroes hairy
	Some like them debonair,
Some prefer a curate
	And some an A.D.C.,
Some like a tough to treat 'em rough,
	But you're my cup of tea.

Some are mad on Airedales
	And some on Pekinese,
On tabby cats or parrots
	Or guinea pigs or geese.
There are patients in asylums
	Who think that they're a tree;
I had an aunt who loved a plant,
	But you're my cup of tea.

Some have sagging waistlines
	And some a bulbous nose
And some a floating kidney
	And some have hammer toes,
Some have tennis elbow
	And some have housemaid's knee,
And some I know have got B.O.,
	But you're my cup of tea.

The blackbird loves the earthworm,
	The adder loves the sun,
The polar bear an iceberg,
	The elephant a bun,
The trout enjoys the river,
	The whale enjoys the sea,
And dogs love most an old lamp-post,
	But you're my cup of tea.

Underneath the Abject Willow

(for Benjamin Britten)

Underneath the abject willow,
    Lover, sulk no more;
Act from thought should quickly follow:
    What is thinking for?
Your unique and moping station
    Proves you cold;
    Stand up and fold
Your map of desolation.

Bells that toll across the meadows
    From the sombre spire,
Toll for those unloving shadows
    Love does not require.
All that lives may love; why longer
    Bow to loss
    With arms across?
Strike and you shall conquer.

Geese in flocks above you flying
    Their direction know;
Brooks beneath the thin ice flowing
    To their oceans go;
Coldest love will warm to action,
    Walk then, come,
    No longer numb,
Into your satisfaction.

Fish in the Unruffled Lakes

Fish in the unruffled lakes
The swarming colours wear,
Swans in the winter air
A white perfection have,
And the great lion walks
Through his innocent grove;
Lion, fish, and swan
Act, and are gone
Upon Time's toppling wave.

We till shadowed days are done,
We must weep and sing
Duty's conscious wrong,
The devil in the clock,
The Goodness carefully worn
For atonement or for luck;
We must lose our loves,
On each breast and bird that moves
Turn an envious look.

Sighs for folly said and done
Twist our narrow days;
But I must bless, I must praise
That you, my swan, who have
All gifts that to the swan
Impulsive Nature gave,
The majesty and pride,
Last night should add
Your voluntary love.

Song

>   The chimney sweepers
> Wash their faces and forget to wash the neck;
>   The lighthouse keepers
> Let the lamps go out and leave the ships to wreck;
>   The prosperous baker
> Leaves the rolls in hundreds in the oven to burn;
>   The undertaker
> Pins a small note on the coffin saying 'Wait till I return,
>   I've got a date with Love.'
>
>   And deep-sea divers
> Cut their boots off and come bubbling to the top,
>   And engine-drivers
> Bring expresses in the tunnel to a stop;
>   The village rector
> Dashes down the side-aisle half-way through a psalm;
>   The sanitary inspector
> Runs off with the cover of the cesspool on his arm –
>   To keep his date with Love.

At Last the Secret Is Out

> At last the secret is out, as it always must come in the
>   end,
> The delicious story is ripe to tell to the intimate friend;
> Over the tea-cups and in the square the tongue has its
>   desire;
> Still waters run deep, my dear, there's never smoke
>   without fire.

Behind the corpse in the reservoir, behind the links,
Behind the lady who dances and the man wi drinks,
Under the look of fatigue, the attack of migraine sigh
There is always another story, there is more than m the eye.

For the clear voice suddenly singing, high up in the convent wall,
The scent of the elder bushes, the sporting prints in the hall,
The croquet matches in summer, the handshake, the cough, the kiss,
There is always a wicked secret, a private reason for this.

Funeral Blues

Stop all the clocks, cut off the telephone,
Prevent the dog from barking with a juicy bone,
Silence the pianos and with muffled drum
Bring out the coffin, let the mourners come.

Let aeroplanes circle moaning overhead
Scribbling in the sky the message He Is Dead,
Put crêpe bows round the white necks of the public doves,
Let the traffic policemen wear black cotton gloves.

He was my North, my South, my East and West,
My working week and my Sunday rest,
My noon, my midnight, my talk, my song;
I thought that love would last for ever: I was wrong.

The stars are not wanted now; put out every one,
Pack up the moon and dismantle the sun,
Pour away the ocean and sweep up the wood;
For nothing now can ever come to any good.

Jam Tart

I'm a jam tart, I'm a bargain basement,
I'm a work of art, I'm a magic casement,
A coal cellar, an umbrella, a sewing machine,
A radio, a hymn book, an old french bean,
The Royal Scot, a fairy grot, a storm at sea, a tram –
      I don't know what I am,
      You've cast a spell on me.

I'm a dog's nose, I'm Sir Humphry Davy,
I'm a Christmas rose, I'm the British Navy,
A motor, a bloater, a charcoal grill,
An octopus, a towpath, Hindenburg's will,
A village fair, a maiden's prayer, the BBC, a pram –
      I don't know what I am,
      You've cast a spell on me.

I'm a salmon, I'm a starting pistol,
I'm backgammon, I'm the Port of Bristol.
A *Times* leader, a child's feeder, an aspirin,
The Ritz Hotel, a boy scout, the wages of sin,
A shaving brush, a schoolgirl's crush, the letter B, a ham –
      I don't know what I am,
      You've cast a spell on me.

I'm an off-break, I'm a clump of beeches,
I'm a tummy ache, I'm Mussolini's speeches,
I'm Balmoral, I'm a sorrel mare, I'm a tug

A cigarette, an organ, a big bed-bug
A traffic sign, a rubber mine, a coffee tree, O damn –
     I don't know what I am,
     You've cast a spell on me.

Death's Echo

'O who can ever gaze his fill',
     Farmer and fisherman say,
'On native shore and local hill,
 Grudge aching limb or callus on the hand?
Fathers, grandfathers stood upon this land,
And here the pilgrims from our loins shall stand.'
     So farmer and fisherman say
     In their fortunate heyday:
     But Death's soft answer drifts across
     Empty catch or harvest loss
       Or an unlucky May.

The earth is an oyster with nothing inside it
     Not to be born is the best for man
The end of toil is a bailiff's order
     Throw down the mattock and dance while you can.

'O life's too short for friends who share',
     Travellers think in their hearts,
'The city's common bed, the air,
 The mountain bivouac and the bathing beach,
Where incidents draw every day from each
Memorable gesture and witty speech.'
     So travellers think in their hearts,
     Till malice or circumstance parts
     Them from their constant humour:
     And shyly Death's coercive rumour
       In the silence starts.

A friend is the old old tale of Narcissus
    Not to be born is the best for man
An active partner in something disgraceful
    Change your partner, dance while you can.

'O stretch your hands across the sea,'
    The impassioned lover cries,
'Stretch them towards your harm and me.
 Our grass is green, and sensual our brief bed,
 The stream sings at its foot, and at its head
 The mild and vegetarian beasts are fed.'
    So the impassioned lover cries
    Till his storm of pleasure dies:
    From the bedpost and the rocks
    Death's enticing echo mocks,
        And his voice replies.

The greater the love, the more false to its object
    Not to be born is the best for man
After the kiss comes the impulse to throttle
    Break the embraces, dance while you can.

'I see the guilty world forgiven,'
    Dreamer and drunkard sing,
'The ladders let down out of heaven;
 The laurel springing from the martyrs' blood;
 The children skipping where the weepers stood;
 The lovers natural, and the beasts all good.'
    So dreamer and drunkard sing
    Till day their sobriety bring:
    Parrotwise with death's reply
    From whelping fear and nesting lie,
        Woods and their echoes ring.

The desires of the heart are as crooked as corkscrews
Not to be born is the best for man
The second best is a formal order
The dance's pattern, dance while you can.
Dance, dance, for the figure is easy
The tune is catching and will not stop
Dance till the stars come down with the rafters
Dance, dance, dance till you drop.

Lullaby

Lay your sleeping head, my love,
Human on my faithless arm;
Time and fevers burn away
Individual beauty from
Thoughtful children, and the grave
Proves the child ephemeral:
But in my arms till break of day
Let the living creature lie,
Mortal, guilty, but to me
The entirely beautiful.

Soul and body have no bounds:
To lovers as they lie upon
Her tolerant enchanted slope
In their ordinary swoon,
Grave the vision Venus sends
Of supernatural sympathy,
Universal love and hope;
While an abstract insight wakes
Among the glaciers and the rocks
The hermit's sensual ecstasy.

Certainty, fidelity
On the stroke of midnight pass
Like vibrations of a bell,
And fashionable madmen raise
Their pedantic boring cry:
Every farthing of the cost,
All the dreaded cards foretell,
Shall be paid, but from this night
Not a whisper, not a thought,
Not a kiss nor look be lost.

Beauty, midnight, vision dies:
Let the winds of dawn that blow
Softly round your dreaming head
Such a day of sweetness show
Eye and knocking heart may bless,
Find the mortal world enough;
Noons of dryness see you fed
By the involuntary powers,
Nights of insult let you pass
Watched by every human love.

Danse Macabre

It's farewell to the drawing-room's civilized cry,
The professor's sensible whereto and why,
The frock-coated diplomat's social aplomb,
Now matters are settled with gas and with bomb.

The works for two pianos, the brilliant stories
Of reasonable giants and remarkable fairies,
The pictures, the ointments, the frangible wares
And the branches of olive are stored upstairs.

For the Devil has broken parole and arisen,
He has dynamited his way out of prison,
Out of the well where his Papa throws
The rebel angel, the outcast rose.

Like influenza he walks abroad,
He stands by the bridge, he waits by the ford,
As a goose or a gull he flies overhead,
He hides in the cupboard and under the bed.

Assuming such shapes as may best disguise
The hate that burns in his big blue eyes;
He may be a baby that croons in its pram,
Or a dear old grannie boarding a tram.

A plumber, a doctor, for he has skill
To adopt a serious profession at will;
Superb at ice-hockey, a prince at the dance,
He's fierce as the tigers, secretive as plants.

O were he to triumph, dear heart, you know
To what depths of shame he would drag you low;
He would steal you away from me, yes, my dear,
He would steal you and cut off your beautiful hair.

Millions already have come to their harm,
Succumbing like doves to his adder's charm;
Hundreds of trees in the wood are unsound:
I'm the axe that must cut them down to the ground.

For I, after all, am the Fortunate One,
The Happy-Go-Lucky, the spoilt Third Son;
For me it is written the Devil to chase
And to rid the earth of the human race.

The behaving of man is a world of horror,
A sedentary Sodom and slick Gomorrah;
I must take charge of the liquid fire
And storm the cities of human desire.

The buying and selling, the eating and drinking,
The disloyal machines and irreverent thinking,
The lovely dullards again and again
Inspiring their bitter ambitious men.

I shall come, I shall punish, the Devil be dead,
I shall have caviare thick on my bread,
I shall build myself a cathedral for home
With a vacuum cleaner in every room.

I shall ride the parade in a platinum car,
My features shall shine, my name shall be Star,
Day-long and night-long the bells I shall peal,
And down the long street I shall turn the cartwheel.

So Little John, Long John, Peter and Paul,
And poor little Horace with only one ball,
You shall leave your breakfast, your desk and your play
On a fine summer morning the Devil to slay.

For it's order and trumpet and anger and drum
And power and glory command you to come;
The graves shall fly open and let you all in,
And the earth shall be emptied of mortal sin.

The fishes are silent deep in the sea,
The skies are lit up like a Christmas tree,
The star in the West shoots its warning cry:
'Mankind is alive, but Mankind must die.'

So good-bye to the house with its wallpaper red,
Good-bye to the sheets on the warm double bed,
Good-bye to the beautiful birds on the wall,
It's good-bye, dear heart, good-bye to you all.

Blues

(for Hedli Anderson)

Ladies and gentlemen, sitting here,
Eating and drinking and warming a chair,
Feeling and thinking and drawing your breath,
Who's sitting next to you? It may be Death.

As a high-stepping blondie with eyes of blue
In the subway, on beaches, Death looks at you;
And married or single or young or old,
You'll become a sugar daddy and do as you're told.

Death is a G-man. You may think yourself smart,
But he'll send you to the hot-seat or plug you through
     the heart;
He may be a slow worker, but in the end
He'll get you for the crime of being born, my friend.

Death as a doctor has first-class degrees;
The world is on his panel; he charges no fees;
He listens to your chest, says – 'You're breathing. That's
     bad.
But don't worry; we'll soon see to that, my lad.'

Death knocks at your door selling real estate,
The value of which will not depreciate;
It's easy, it's convenient, it's old world. You'll sign,
Whatever your income, on the dotted line.

Death as a teacher is simply grand;
The dumbest pupil can understand.
He has only one subject and that is the Tomb;
But no one ever yawns or asks to leave the room.

So whether you're standing broke in the rain,
Or playing poker or drinking champagne,
Death's looking for you, he's already on the way,
So look out for him tomorrow or perhaps today.

Give Up Love

Cleopatra, Anthony
Were introspective you'll agree,
Got in a morbid state because
They lounged about too much indoors.
If they'd gone in for Eton Fives
They wouldn't have gone and lost their lives.

For if you love sport then you won't give a thought
    To all that goes on in the park.
Learning to bowl will keep your heart whole,
    You won't want to go out after dark.
Love is unenglish and sloppy and soft
    So be English and stringy and tough.
If you keep yourself fit you will never want It,
        So give up Love.

Abelard and Heloise
Were a pair of sentimental geese.
They ought to have taken exercise,
Not spent their time in sighs and cries.
Gone in for netball or sailing boats
Instead of writing sloppy notes.

For if you can jump then you won't want to bump
    By mistake into girls in the park.
If you can dive you won't yearn for High Life,
    You won't want to go out after dark.
Love is unenglish and sloppy and soft
    So be English and stringy and tough.
If you hole out in one, then love seems poor fun,
        So give up Love.

Dante wrote a lot of slush
Because he got an unhealthy crush
On Beatrice who was dead to him.
He ought to have kept himself in trim
Upon the horizontal bars,
Not written tripe about the stars.

For if you keep a straight bat then love will seem flat
    It won't tempt you to spoon in the park,
If your backhand's like this, then you won't want to kiss,
    You won't want to go out after dark.
Love is unenglish and sloppy and soft
    So be English and stringy and tough.
You won't feel the loss if you're good at lacrosse
      So give up Love.

Don Juan was another one
For whom something should have been done.
Compulsory games would have been the cure
For his nasty Spanish habits I'm sure.
Had someone seen that he played cricket
He would not have been so wicked.

For if you play games you will never write names
    On seats in the public park.
Riding to hounds puts love out of bounds,
    You won't want to go out after dark.
Love is unenglish and sloppy and soft
    So be English and stringy and tough.
Love makes you laugh if you play centre half
      So give up Love.

Nonsense Song

My love is like a red red rose
Or concerts for the blind,
She's like a mutton-chop before
And a rifle-range behind.

Her hair is like a looking-glass,
Her brow is like a bog,
Her eyes are like a flock of sheep
Seen through a London fog.

Her nose is like an Irish jig,
Her mouth is like a 'bus,
Her chin is like a bowl of soup
Shared between all of us.

Her form divine is like a map
Of the United States,
Her foot is like a motor-car
Without its number-plates.

No steeple-jack shall part us now
Nor fireman in a frock;
True love could sink a Channel boat
Or knit a baby's sock.

Johnny

O the valley in the summer where I and my John
Beside the deep river would walk on and on
While the flowers at our feet and the birds up above
Argued so sweetly on reciprocal love,
And I leaned on his shoulder; 'O Johnny, let's play':
But he frowned like thunder and he went away.

O that Friday near Christmas as I well recall
When we went to the Charity Matinee Ball,
The floor was so smooth and the band was so loud
And Johnny so handsome I felt so proud;
'Squeeze me tighter, dear Johnny, let's dance till it's day':
But he frowned like thunder and he went away.

Shall I ever forget at the Grand Opera
When music poured out of each wonderful star?
Diamonds and pearls they hung dazzling down
Over each silver or golden silk gown;
'O John I'm in heaven', I whispered to say:
But he frowned like thunder and he went away.

O but he was as fair as a garden in flower,
As slender and tall as the great Eiffel Tower,
When the waltz throbbed out on the long promenade
O his eyes and his smile they went straight to my heart;
'O marry me, Johnny, I'll love and obey':
But he frowned like thunder and he went away.

O last night I dreamed of you, Johnny, my lover,
You'd the sun on one arm and the moon on the other,
The sea it was blue and the grass it was green,
Every star rattled a round tambourine;
Ten thousand miles deep in a pit there I lay:
But you frowned like thunder and you went away.

Miss Gee

Let me tell you a little story
    About Miss Edith Gee;
She lived in Clevedon Terrace
    At Number 83.

She'd a slight squint in her left eye,
    Her lips they were thin and small,
She had narrow sloping shoulders
    And she had no bust at all.

She'd a velvet hat with trimmings,
    And a dark-grey serge costume;
She lived in Clevedon Terrace
    In a small bed-sitting room.

She'd a purple mac for wet days,
    A green umbrella too to take,
She'd a bicycle with shopping basket
    And a harsh back-pedal brake.

The Church of Saint Aloysius
    Was not so very far;
She did a lot of knitting,
    Knitting for that Church Bazaar.

Miss Gee looked up at the starlight
    And said: 'Does anyone care
That I live in Clevedon Terrace
    On one hundred pounds a year?'

She dreamed a dream one evening
    That she was the Queen of France
And the Vicar of Saint Aloysius
    Asked Her Majesty to dance.

But a storm blew down the palace,
    She was biking through a field of corn,
And a bull with the face of the Vicar
    Was charging with lowered horn.

She could not feel his hot breath behind her,
    He was going to overtake;
And the bicycle went slower and slower
    Because of that back-pedal brake.

Summer made the trees a picture,
  Winter made them a wreck;
She bicycled to the evening service
  With her clothes buttoned up to her neck.

She passed by the loving couples,
  She turned her head away;
She passed by the loving couples
  And they didn't ask her to stay.

Miss Gee sat down in the side-aisle,
  She heard the organ play;
And the choir it sang so sweetly
  At the ending of the day.

Miss Gee knelt down in the side-aisle,
  She knelt down on her knees;
'Lead me not into temptation
  But make me a good girl, please.'

The days and nights went by her
  Like waves round a Cornish wreck;
She bicycled down to the doctor
  With her clothes buttoned up to her neck.

She bicycled down to the doctor,
  And rang the surgery bell;
'O, doctor, I've a pain inside me,
  And I don't feel very well.'

Doctor Thomas looked her over,
  And then he looked some more;
Walked over to his wash-basin,
  Said: 'Why didn't you come before?'

Doctor Thomas sat over his dinner,
  Though his wife was waiting to ring;
Rolling his bread into pellets,
  Said: 'Cancer's a funny thing.

'Nobody knows what the cause is,
    Though some pretend they do;
It's like some hidden assassin
    Waiting to strike at you.

'Childless women get it,
    And men when they retire;
It's as if there had to be some outlet
    For their foiled creative fire.'

His wife she rang for the servant,
    Said: 'Don't be so morbid, dear';
He said: 'I saw Miss Gee this evening
    And she's a goner, I fear.'

They took Miss Gee to the hospital,
    She lay there a total wreck,
Lay in the ward for women
    With the bedclothes right up to her neck.

They laid her on the table,
    The students began to laugh;
And Mr Rose the surgeon
    He cut Miss Gee in half.

Mr Rose he turned to his students,
    Said: 'Gentlemen, if you please,
We seldom see a sarcoma
    As far advanced as this.'

They took her off the table,
    They wheeled away Miss Gee
Down to another department
    Where they study Anatomy.

They hung her from the ceiling,
    Yes, they hung up Miss Gee;
And a couple of Oxford Groupers
    Carefully dissected her knee.

Victor

Victor was a little baby,
        Into this world he came;
His father took him on his knee and said:
        'Don't dishonour the family name.'

Victor looked up at his father
        Looked up with big round eyes;
His father said: 'Victor, my only son,
        Don't you ever tell lies.'

Victor and his father went riding
        Out in a little dog-cart;
His father took a Bible from his pocket and read:
        'Blessed are the pure in heart.'

It was a frosty December,
        It wasn't the season for fruits;
His father fell dead of heart disease
        While lacing up his boots.

It was a frosty December
        When into his grave he sank;
His uncle found Victor a post as cashier
        In the Midland Counties Bank.

It was a frosty December
        Victor was only eighteen,
But his figures were neat and his margins straight
        And his cuffs were always clean.

He took a room at the Peveril,
        A respectable boarding-house;
And Time watched Victor day after day
        As a cat will watch a mouse.

The clerks slapped Victor on the shoulder;
  'Have you ever had a woman?' they said,
'Come down town with us on Saturday night.'
  Victor smiled and shook his head.

The manager sat in his office,
  Smoked a Corona cigar;
Said: 'Victor's a decent fellow but
  He's too mousey to go far.'

Victor went up to his bedroom,
  Set the alarum bell;
Climbed into bed, took his Bible and read
  Of what happened to Jezebel.

It was the First of April,
  Anna to the Peveril came;
Her eyes, her lips, her breasts, her hips
  And her smile set men aflame.

She looked as pure as a schoolgirl
  On her First Communion day,
But her kisses were like the best champagne
  When she gave herself away.

It was the Second of April,
  She was wearing a coat of fur;
Victor met her upon the stairs
  And he fell in love with her.

The first time he made his proposal,
  She laughed, said: 'I'll never wed';
The second time there was a pause,
  Then she smiled and shook her head.

Anna looked into her mirror,
  Pouted and gave a frown;
Said: 'Victor's as dull as a wet afternoon
  But I've got to settle down.'

The third time he made his proposal,
        As they walked by the Reservoir,
She gave him a kiss like a blow on the head,
        Said: 'You are my heart's desire.'

They were married early in August,
        She said: 'Kiss me, you funny boy';
Victor took her in his arms and said:
        'O my Helen of Troy.'

It was the middle of September,
        Victor came to the office one day;
He was wearing a flower in his buttonhole,
        He was late but he was gay.

The clerks were talking of Anna,
        The door was just ajar;
One said: 'Poor old Victor, but where ignorance
        Is bliss, etcetera.'

Victor stood still as a statue,
        The door was just ajar;
One said: 'God, what fun I had with her
        In that Baby Austin car.'

Victor walked out into the High Street,
        He walked to the edge of the town;
He came to the allotments and the rubbish heaps
        And his tears came tumbling down.

Victor looked up at the sunset
        As he stood there all alone;
Cried: 'Are you in Heaven, Father?'
        But the sky said 'Address not known.'

Victor looked up at the mountains,
        The mountains all covered with snow;
Cried: 'Are you pleased with me, Father?'
        And the answer came back, 'No.'

Victor came to the forest,
>> Cried: 'Father, will she ever be true?'
And the oaks and the beeches shook their heads
>> And they answered: 'Not to you.'

Victor came to the meadow
>> Where the wind went sweeping by;
Cried: 'O Father, I love her so',
>> But the wind said: 'She must die.'

Victor came to the river
>> Running so deep and so still;
Crying: 'O Father, what shall I do?'
>> And the river answered: 'Kill.'

Anna was sitting at table,
>> Drawing cards from a pack;
Anna was sitting at table
>> Waiting for her husband to come back.

It wasn't the Jack of Diamonds
>> Nor the Joker she drew at first;
It wasn't the King or the Queen of Hearts
>> But the Ace of Spades reversed.

Victor stood in the doorway,
>> He didn't utter a word;
She said: 'What's the matter, darling?'
>> He behaved as if he hadn't heard.

There was a voice in his left ear,
>> There was a voice in his right,
There was a voice at the base of his skull
>> Saying: 'She must die tonight.'

Victor picked up a carving-knife,
>> His features were set and drawn,
Said: 'Anna, it would have been better for you
>> If you had not been born.'

Anna jumped up from the table,
       Anna started to scream,
But Victor came slowly after her
       Like a horror in a dream.

She dodged behind the sofa,
       She tore down a curtain rod,
But Victor came slowly after her,
       Said: 'Prepare to meet thy God.'

She managed to wrench the door open,
       She ran and she didn't stop.
But Victor followed her up the stairs
       And he caught her at the top.

He stood there above the body,
       He stood there holding the knife;
And the blood ran down the stairs and sang:
       'I'm the Resurrection and the Life.'

They tapped Victor on the shoulder,
       They took him away in a van;
He sat as quiet as a lump of moss
       Saying: 'I am the Son of Man.'

Victor sat in a corner
       Making a woman of clay,
Saying: 'I am Alpha and Omega, I shall come
       To judge the earth one day.'

James Honeyman

James Honeyman was a silent child
He didn't laugh or cry;
He looked at his mother
With curiosity.

Mother came up to the nursery,
Peeped through the open door,
Saw him striking matches
Sitting on the nursery floor.

He went to the children's party,
The buns were full of cream;
Sat dissolving sugar
In his teacup in a dream.

On his eighth birthday
Didn't care that the day was wet
For by his bedside
Lay a ten-shilling chemistry set.

Teacher said: 'James Honeyman's
The cleverest boy we've had,
But he doesn't play with the others
And that, I think, is sad.'

While the other boys played football
He worked in the laboratory
Got a scholarship to college,
And a first-class degree.

Kept awake with black coffee,
Took to wearing glasses,
Writing a thesis
On the toxic gases.

Went out into the country,
Went by a Green Line Bus,
Walked on the Chilterns,
Thought about Phosphorus.

Said: 'Lewisite in its day
Was pretty decent stuff,
But under modern conditions
It's not nearly strong enough.'

His Tutor sipped his port,
Said: 'I think it's clear
That young James Honeyman's
The most brilliant man of his year.'

He got a job in research
With Imperial Alkali,
Said to himself while shaving:
'I'll be famous before I die.'

His landlady said: 'Mr Honeyman,
You've only got one life,
You ought to have some fun, Sir.
You ought to find a wife.'

At Imperial Alkali
There was a girl called Doreen,
One day she cut her finger,
Asked him for iodine.

'I'm feeling faint,' she said.
He led her to a chair,
Fetched her a glass of water,
Wanted to stroke her hair.

They took a villa on the Great West Road,
Painted green and white;
On her left a United Dairy,
A cinema on their right.

At the bottom of his garden
He built a little shed.
'He's going to blow us up',
All the neighbours said.

Doreen called down at midnight:
'Jim dear, it's time for bed.'
'I'll finish my experiment
And then I'll come,' he said.

Caught influenza at Christmas,
The Doctor said: 'Go to bed.'
'I'll finish my experiment
And then I'll go,' he said.

Walked out on Sundays,
Helped to push the pram,
Said: 'I'm looking for a gas, dear;
A whiff will kill a man.

'I'm going to find it,
That's what I'm going to do.'
Doreen squeezed his hand and said:
'Jim, I believe in you.'

In the hot nights of summer
When the roses all were red
James Honeyman was working
In his little garden shed.

Came upstairs at midnight,
Kissed his sleeping son,
Held up a sealed glass test-tube,
Said: 'Look, Doreen, I've won!'

They stood together by the window,
The moon was bright and clear.
He said: 'At last I've done something
That's worthy of you, dear.'

Took a train next morning,
Went up to Whitehall
With the phial in his pocket
To show it to them all.

Sent in his card,
The officials only swore:
'Tell him we're very busy
And show him the door.'

Doreen said to the neighbours:
'Isn't it a shame?
My husband's so clever
And they didn't know his name.'

One neighbour was sympathetic,
Her name was Mrs Flower.
She was the agent
Of a foreign power.

One evening they sat at supper,
There came a gentle knock:
'A gentleman to see Mr Honeyman.'
He stayed till eleven o'clock.

They walked down the garden together,
Down to the little shed:
'We'll see you, then, in Paris.
Good night', the gentleman said.

The boat was nearing Dover,
He looked back at Calais:
Said: 'Honeyman's N.P.C.
Will be heard of, some day.'

He was sitting in the garden
Writing notes on a pad,
Their little son was playing
Round his mother and dad.

Suddenly from the east
Some aeroplanes appeared,
Somebody screamed: 'They're bombers!
War must have been declared!'

The first bomb hit the Dairy,
The second the cinema,
The third fell in the garden
Just like a falling star.

'Oh kiss me, Mother, kiss me,
And tuck me up in bed
For Daddy's invention
Is going to choke me dead!'

'Where are you, James, where are you?
Oh put your arms round me,
For my lungs are full
Of Honeyman's N.P.C.!'

'I wish I were a salmon
Swimming in the sea,
I wish I were the dove
That coos upon the tree.'

'Oh you are not a salmon,
Oh you are not a dove;
But you invented the vapour
That is killing those you love.'

'Oh hide me in the mountains,
Oh drown me in the sea.
Lock me in the dungeon
And throw away the key.'

'Oh you can't hide in the mountains,
Oh you can't drown in the sea,
But you must die, and you know why,
By Honeyman's N.P.C.!'

Roman Wall Blues

Over the heather the wet wind blows,
I've lice in my tunic and a cold in my nose.

The rain comes pattering out of the sky,
I'm a Wall soldier, I don't know why.

The mist creeps over the hard grey stone,
My girl's in Tungria; I sleep alone.

Aulus goes hanging around her place,
I don't like his manners, I don't like his face.

Piso's a Christian, he worships a fish;
There'd be no kissing if he had his wish.

She gave me a ring but I diced it away;
I want my girl and I want my pay.

When I'm a veteran with only one eye
I shall do nothing but look at the sky.

As I Walked Out One Evening

As I walked out one evening,
    Walking down Bristol Street,
The crowds upon the pavement
    Were fields of harvest wheat.

And down by the brimming river
    I heard a lover sing
Under an arch of the railway:
    'Love has no ending.

'I'll love you, dear, I'll love you
    Till China and Africa meet
And the river jumps over the mountain
    And the salmon sing in the street.

'I'll love you till the ocean
    Is folded and hung up to dry
And the seven stars go squawking
    Like geese about the sky.

'The years shall run like rabbits
    For in my arms I hold
The Flower of the Ages
    And the first love of the world.'

But all the clocks in the city
    Began to whirr and chime:
'O let not Time deceive you,
    You cannot conquer Time.

'In the burrows of the Nightmare
    Where Justice naked is,
Time watches from the shadow
    An coughs when you would kiss.

'In headaches and in worry
    Vaguely life leaks away,
And Time will have his fancy
    Tomorrow or today.

'Into many a green valley
    Drifts the appalling snow;
Time breaks the threaded dances
    And the diver's brilliant bow.

'O plunge your hands in water,
    Plunge them in up to the wrist;
Stare, stare in the basin
    And wonder what you've missed.

'The glacier knocks in the cupboard,
    The desert sighs in the bed,
And the crack in the tea-cup opens
    A lane to the land of the dead.

'Where the beggars raffle the banknotes
    And the Giant is enchanting to Jack,
And the Lily-white Boy is a Roarer
    And Jill goes down on her back.

'O look, look in the mirror,
    O look in your distress;
Life remains a blessing
    Although you cannot bless.

'O stand, stand at the window
    As the tears scald and start;
You shall love your crooked neighbour
    With your crooked heart.'

It was late, late in the evening,
    The lovers they were gone;
The clocks had ceased their chiming
    And the deep river ran on.

O Tell Me the Truth About Love

Some say that Love's a little boy
    And some say he's a bird,
Some say he makes the world go round
    And some say that's absurd:
But when I asked the man next door
    Who looked as if he knew,
His wife was very cross indeed
    And said it wouldn't do.

Does it look like a pair of pyjamas
    Or the ham in a temperance hotel,
Does its odour remind one of llamas
    Or has it a comforting smell?
Is it prickly to touch as a hedge is
    Or soft as eiderdown fluff,
Is it sharp or quite smooth at the edges?
    O tell me the truth about love.

The history books refer to it
        In cryptic little notes,
And it's a common topic on
        The Trans-Atlantic boats;
I've found the subject mentioned in
        Accounts of suicides,
And even seen it scribbled on
        The backs of railway guides.

Does it howl like a hungry Alsatian
        Or boom like a military band,
Could one give a first-class imitation
        On a saw or a Steinway Grand,
Is its singing at parties a riot,
        Does it only like Classical stuff,
Will it stop when one wants to be quiet?
        O tell me the truth about love.

I looked inside the summer-house,
        It wasn't ever there,
I've tried the Thames at Maidenhead
        And Brighton's bracing air;
I don't know what the blackbird sang
        Or what the roses said,
But it wasn't in the chicken-run
        Or underneath the bed.

Can it pull extraordinary faces,
        Is it usually sick on a swing,
Does it spend all its time at the races
        Or fiddling with pieces of string,
Has it views of its own about money,
        Does it think Patriotism enough,
Are its stories vulgar but funny?
        O tell me the truth about love.

Your feelings when you meet it, I
     Am told you can't forget,
I've sought it since I was a child
     But haven't found it yet;
I'm getting on for thirty-five,
     And still I do not know
What kind of creature it can be
     That bothers people so.

When it comes, will it come without warning
     Just as I'm picking my nose,
Will it knock on my door in the morning
     Or tread in the bus on my toes,
Will it come like a change in the weather,
     Will its greeting be courteous or bluff,
Will it alter my life altogether?
     O tell me the truth about love.

Gare du Midi

A nondescript express in from the South,
Crowds round the ticket barrier, a face
To welcome which the mayor has not contrived
Bugles or braid: something about the mouth
Distracts the stray look with alarm and pity.
Snow is falling. Clutching a little case,
He walks out briskly to infect a city
Whose terrible future may have just arrived.

Epitaph on a Tyrant

Perfection, of a kind, was what he was after,
And the poetry he invented was easy to understand;
He knew human folly like the back of his hand,

And was greatly interested in armies and fleets;
When he laughed, respectable senators burst with
     laughter,
And when he cried the little children died in the streets.

The Unknown Citizen

To JS/07/M/378
This Marble Monument is Erected by the State

He was found by the Bureau of Statistics to be
One against whom there was no official complaint,
And all the reports on his conduct agree
That, in the modern sense of an old-fashioned word, he
     was a saint,
For in everything he did he served the Greater Community.
Except for the War till the day he retired
He worked in a factory and never got fired,
But satisfied his employers, Fudge Motors Inc.
Yet he wasn't a scab or odd in his views,
For his Union reports that he paid his dues,
(Our report on his Union shows it was sound)
And our Social Psychology workers found
That he was popular with his mates and liked a drink.
The Press are convinced that he bought a paper every day
And that his reactions to advertisements were normal in
     every way.
Policies taken out in his name prove that he was fully
     insured,
And his Health-card shows he was once in hospital but
     left it cured.
Both Producers Research and High-Grade Living declare
He was fully sensible to the advantages of the
     Installment Plan
And had everything necessary to the Modern Man,
A gramophone, a radio, a car and a frigidaire.

Our researchers into Public Opinion are content
That he held the proper opinions for the time of year;
When there was peace, he was for peace; when there
     was war, he went.
He was married and added five children to the population,
Which our Eugenist says was the right number for a
     parent of his generation,
And our teachers report that he never interfered with
     their education.
Was he free? Was he happy? The question is absurd:
Had anything been wrong, we should certainly have
     heard.

Refugee Blues

Say this city has ten million souls,
Some are living in mansions, some are living in holes:
Yet there's no place for us, my dear, yet there's no place
     for us.

Once we had a country and we thought it fair,
Look in the atlas and you'll find it there:
We cannot go there now, my dear, we cannot go there
     now.

In the village churchyard there grows an old yew,
Every spring it blossoms anew:
Old passports can't do that, my dear, old passports can't
     do that.

The consul banged the table and said;
'If you've got no passport you're officially dead:'
But we are still alive, my dear, but we are still alive.

Went to a committee; they offered me a chair;
Asked me politely to return next year:
But where shall we go to-day, my dear, but where shall
we go to-day?

Came to a public meeting; the speaker got up and said;
'If we let them in, they will steal our daily bread':
He was talking of you and me, my dear, he was talking
of you and me.

Thought I heard the thunder rumbling in the sky;
It was Hitler over Europe, saying: 'They must die':
O we were in his mind, my dear, O we were in his
mind.

Saw a poodle in a jacket fastened with a pin,
Saw a door opened and a cat let in:
But they weren't German Jews, my dear, but they
weren't German Jews.

Went down the harbour and stood upon the quay,
Saw the fish swimming as if they were free:
Only ten feet away, my dear, only ten feet away.

Walked through a wood, saw the birds in the trees;
They had no politicians and sang at their ease:
They weren't the human race, my dear, they weren't the
human race.

Dreamed I saw a building with a thousand floors,
A thousand windows and a thousand doors:
Not one of them was ours, my dear, not one of them
was ours.

Stood on a great plain in the falling snow;
Ten thousand soldiers marched to and fro:
Looking for you and me, my dear, looking for you and
me.

Ode

In this epoch of high-pressure selling
    When the salesman gives us no rest,
And even Governments are yelling
    'Our Brand is Better than Best';
When the hoardings announce a new diet
    To take all our odour away,
Or a medicine to keep the kids quiet,
    Or a belt that will give us S. A.,
Or a soap to wash shirts in a minute,
    One wonders at times, I'm afraid,
If there is one word of truth in it,
    And how much the writers were paid.

O is there a technique to praise the
    HOTEL GEORGE WASHINGTON then,
That doesn't resemble the ways the
    Really professional men
Convince a two-hundred-pound matron
    She's the feather she was in her youth?
Well, considering who is patron,
    I think I shall stick to the truth.
It stands on the Isle of Manhattan,
    Not far from the Lexington line,
And although it's démodé to fatten,
    There's a ballroom where parties may dine.

The walls look unlikely to crumble
    And although, to be perfectly fair,
A few entomologists grumble
    That bugs are exceedingly rare,
The Normal Man life is so rich in
    Will not be disgusted, perhaps,
To learn that there's food in the kitchen,
    And that water comes out of the taps,
That the sheets are not covered with toffee,

And I think he may safely assume
That he won't find a fish in his coffee
    Or a very large snake in his room.

While the curious student may study
    All the sorts and conditions of men,
And distinguish the Bore from the Buddy,
    And the Fowl from the Broody Old Hen;
And presently learn to discover
    How one looks when one's deeply in debt,
And which one is in search of a lover,
    And which one is in need of a vet;
And among all these Mrs and Mr's,
    To detect as each couple arrives,
How many are really their sisters,
    And how many are simply their wives.

But now let me add in conclusion
    Just one little personal remark;
Though I know that the Self's an illusion,
    And that words leave us all in the dark,
That we're serious mental cases
    If we think that we think that we know,
Yet I've stayed in hotels in most places
    Where my passport permits me to go
(Excluding the British Dominions
    And Turkey and U.S.S.R.)
And this one, in my humble opinion's
    The nicest I've been in so far.

Calypso

Driver drive faster and make a good run
Down the Springfield Line under the shining sun.

Fly like the aeroplane, don't pull up short
Till you brake for Grand Central Station, New York.

For there in the middle of that waiting hall
Should be standing the one that I love best of all.

If he's not there to meet me when I get to town,
I'll stand on the pavement with tears rolling down.

For he is the one that I love to look on,
The acme of kindness and perfection.

He presses my hand and he says he loves me
Which I find an admirable peculiarity.

The woods are bright green on both sides of the line;
The trees have their loves though they're different from
    mine.

But the poor fat old banker in the sun-parlour car
Has no one to love him except his cigar.

If I were the head of the Church or the State
I'd powder my nose and just tell them to wait.

For love's more important and powerful than
Even a priest or a politician.

Heavy Date

Sharp and silent in the
Clear October lighting
Of a Sunday morning
    The great city lies;
And I at a window
Looking over water
At the world of Business
    With a lover's eyes.

All mankind, I fancy,
When anticipating
Anything exciting
    Like a rendez-vous,
Occupy the time in
Purely random thinking,
For when love is waiting
    Logic will not do.

Much as he would like to
Concentrate completely
On the precious Object,
    Love has not the power:
Goethe put it neatly;
No one cares to watch the
Loveliest sunset after
    Quarter of an hour.

So I pass the time, dear,
Till I see you, writing
Down whatever nonsense
    Comes into my head;
Let the life that has been
Lightly buried in my
Personal Unconscious
    Rise up from the dead.

Why association
Should see fit to see a
Bull-dog by a trombone
    On a grassy plain
Littered with old letters,
Leaves me simply guessing,
I suppose it's La Con-
    -dition Humaine.

As at lantern lectures
Image follows image;
Here comes a steam-roller
    Through an orange grove,
Driven by a nursemaid
As she sadly mutters:
'Zola, poor old Zola
    Murdered by a stove.'

Now I hear Saint Francis
Telling me in breezy
Tones as we are walking
    Near a power-house:
'Loving birds is easy,
Any fool can do it,
But I must admit it's
    Hard to love the louse.'

Malinowski, Rivers,
Benedict and others
Show how common culture
    Shapes and separate lives:
Matrilineal races
Kill their mothers' brothers
In their dreams and turn their
    Sisters into wives.

As an intellectual
Member of the Middle
Classes or what-have-you
    So I have to dream:
Essence without Form is
Free but ineffectual,
Birth and education
    Guide the living stream.

Who when looking over
Faces in the subway,
Each with its uniqueness,
      Would not, did he dare,
Ask what forms exactly
Suited to their weakness
Love and desperation
      Take to govern there.

Would not like to know what
Influence occupation
Has on human vision
      Of the human fate:
Do all clerks for instance
Pigeon-hole creation,
Brokers see the Ding-an-
      -sich as Real Estate?

When a politician
Dreams about his sweetheart,
Does he multiply her
      Face into a crowd,
Are her fond responses
All-or-none reactions,
Does he try to buy her,
      Is the kissing loud?

Strange are love's mutations:
Thus, the early poem
Of the flesh sub rosa
      Has been known to grow
Now and then into the
Amor intellectu-
-alis of Spinoza;
      How we do not know.

Slowly we are learning,
We at least know this much,
That we have to unlearn
    Much that we were taught,
And are growing chary
Of emphatic dogmas;
Love like Matter is much
    Odder than we thought.

Love requires an Object,
But this varies so much,
Almost, I imagine,
    Anything will do:
When I was a child, I
Loved a pumping-engine,
Thought it every bit as
    Beautiful as you.

Love has no position,
Love's a way of living,
One kind of relation
    Possible between
Any things or persons
Given one condition,
The one sine qua non
    Being mutual need.

Through it we discover
An essential secret
Called by some Salvation
    And by some Success;
Crying for the moon is
Naughtiness and envy,
We can only love what-
    -ever we possess.

I believed for years that
Love was the conjunction
Of two oppositions;
        That was all untrue;
Every young man fears that
He is not worth loving:
Bless you, darling, I have
        Found myself in you.

I should love to go on
Telling how I love you,
Thanking you for happy
        Changes in my life,
But it would be silly
Seeing that you know it
And that any moment
        Now you may arrive.

When two lovers meet, then
There's an end of writing
Thought and Analytics:
        Lovers, like the dead,
In their loves are equal;
Sophomores and peasants,
Poets and their critics
        Are the same in bed.

Song

Warm are the still and lucky miles,
White shores of longing stretch away,
The light of recognition fills
        The whole great day, and bright
The tiny world of lovers' arms.

Silence invades the breathing wood
Where drowsy limbs a treasure keep,
Now greenly falls the learned shade
    Across the sleeping brows
And stirs their secret to a smile.

Restored! Returned! The lost are born
On seas of shipwreck home at last:
See! In the fire of praising burns
    The dry dumb past, and we
The life-day long shall part no more.

'Gold in the North' Came the Blizzard to Say

'Gold in the North,' came the blizzard to say,
I left my sweetheart at the break of day,
The gold ran out and my love turned grey.
You don't know all, sir, you don't know all.

'The West,' said the sun, 'for enterprise,'
A bullet in Frisco put me wise,
My last words were 'God damn your eyes.'
You don't know all, sir, you don't know all.

In the streets of New York I was young and swell,
I rode the market, the market fell,
One morning I woke and found myself in hell,
You don't know all, sir, you don't know all.

In Alabama my heart was full,
Down by the river bank I stole,
The waters of grief went over my soul,
You don't know all, ma'am, you don't know all.

    In the saloons I heaved a sigh,
    Lost in deserts of alkali I lay down to die;
    There's always a sorrow can get you down,
    All the world's whiskey won't ever drown.

Some think they're strong, some think they're smart,
Like butterflies they're pulled apart,
America can break your heart.
You don't know all, sir, you don't know all.

The Glamour Boys and Girls Have Grievances Too

Chorus of Film Stars and Models	You've no idea how dull it is
	Just being perfect nullities,
	   The idols of a democratic nation,
	The heroes of a multitude,
	Their dreams of female pulchritude;
	   We're very, very tired of admiration.

Woman Film Star Man Film Star Both	My measurement around the hips,
	The cut of my moustache and lips,
	   Obey the whims of fashion;
	In our embraces we select
	Whatever technique seems correct
	To give the visual effect
	   Of an Eternal Passion.

Female Models
 	
Male Models
 	
Female Models
Male Models
Female Models
	On beaches or in night clubs I
	Excel at femininity.
	   And I at all athletics;
	I pay attention to my hair.
	For personal hygiene I've a flair,
	The Hercules of underwear,
	   The Venus of cosmetics.

Chorus	We're bored with being glamorous,
	We're bored with being amorous,
	   For all our fans we don't give a
	      banana;

Who wants to be exhibited
To all the world's inhibited
    As representative Americana?

Women Film Stars The things a man of eighty-two
Will ask of his dream ingénue
    I shouldn't like to retail.
Unless you've tried to play Mamma,
You can't guess how particular
Young men who miss their mothers are
    About each little detail.

Men Film Stars Rescuing girls from waterfalls,
Or shooting up the sheriff, palls
    Like any violent action.
We never want to die again,
Or throw a custard pie again,
To give the decent citizen
    Vicarious satisfaction.

Quartet of The growth of social consciousness
Film Stars Has failed to make our problems less,
    Indeed, they grow intenser:
And what with Freud and what with
        Marx,
With bureaucrats and matriarchs,
The chances are our little larks
    Will not get past the censor.

You'd hate it if you were employed
To be a sin in celluloid
    Or else a saint in plaster;
O little hearts who make a fuss,
What pleasure it would be to us
To give the bird to Oedipus,
    The raspberry to Jocasta.

Chorus   You've no idea how dull it is
           Just being perfect nullities,
              The idols of a democratic nation,
           The heroes of the multitude,
           Their dreams of female pulchritude;
             We're VERY, VERY tired of
                admiration.

Carry Her Over the Water

Carry her over the water,
   And set her down under the tree,
Where the culvers white all day and all night,
   And the winds from every quarter
Sing agreeably, agreeably, agreeably of love.

Put a gold ring on her finger,
   And press her close to your heart,
While the fish in the lake their snapshots take,
   And the frog, that sanguine singer,
Sings agreeably, agreeably, agreeably of love.

The streets shall all flock to your marriage,
   The houses turn round to look,
The tables and chairs say suitable prayers,
   And the horses drawing your carriage
Sing agreeably, agreeably, agreeably of love.

Eyes Look into the Well

Eyes look into the well,
Tears run down from the eye;
The tower cracked and fell
From the quiet winter sky.

Under the midnight stone
Love was buried by thieves;
The robbed heart begs for a bone,
The damned rustle like leaves.

Face down in the flooded brook
With nothing more to say,
Lies One the soldiers took,
And spoiled and threw away.

Lady Weeping at the Crossroads

Lady, weeping at the crossroads
Would you meet your love
In the twilight with his greyhounds,
And the hawk on his glove?

Bribe the birds then on the branches,
Bribe them to be dumb,
Stare the hot sun out of heaven
That the night may come.

Starless are the nights of travel,
Bleak the winter wind;
Run with terror all before you
And regret behind.

Run until you hear the ocean's
Everlasting cry;
Deep though it may be and bitter
You must drink it dry.

Wear out patience in the lowest
Dungeons of the sea,
Searching through the stranded shipwrecks
For the golden key.

Push onto the world's end, pay the
Dread guard with a kiss;
Cross the rotten bridge that totters
Over the abyss.

There stands the deserted castle
Ready to explore;
Enter, climb the marble staircase
Open the locked door.

Cross the silent empty ballroom,
Doubt and danger past;
Blow the cobwebs from the mirror
See yourself at last.

Put your hand behind the wainscot,
You have done your part;
Find the penknife there and plunge it
Into your false heart.

Notes

Parents once upon a time
Thought that acting was a crime;
'Daughter,' many of them said,
'We would rather see you dead
Than upon a public stage.'
Ours is a more liberal age:
Not a father breaks his heart
If she does Commercial Art,
Not a mother's hair turns grey
If her only son today
Finds an outlet of expression
In the journalist profession.

*

His ageing nature is the same
As when childhood wore its name
In an atmosphere of love
And to itself appeared enough:
Only now when he has come
In walking distance of his tomb,
He at last discovers who
He had always been to whom
He so often was untrue.

*

Infants in their mothers' arms
Exercise their budding charms
On their fingers and their toes,
Striving ever to enclose
In the circle of their will
Objects disobedient still.
But the boy comes soon enough
To the limits of self-love,
And the adult learns how small
Is the individual,
How much stronger is the state
That will not co-operate
With the kingdom of his mind:
All his lifetime he will find
Swollen knee or aching tooth
Hostile to his search for truth;
Never will his sex belong
To his world of right and wrong,
Its libido comprehend
Who is foe and who is friend.

*

Do we want to return to the womb? Not at all.
No one really desires the impossible.
That is only the image out of our past
We practical people use when we cast
Our eyes on the future, to whom freedom is
The absence of all dualities.
Since there never can be much of that for us
In the universe of Copernicus,
Any heaven we think it decent to enter
Must be Ptolemaic with ourselves at the centre.

*

Base words are uttered only by the base
And can, as such, be clearly understood:
But noble platitudes – ah, there's a case
When the most careful scrutiny is needed
To tell the orator who's really good
From one who's base but merely has succeeded.

*

Once for candy cook had stolen
X was punished by Papa;
When he asked where babies came from
He was lied to by Mama.

Now the city streets are waiting
To mislead him, and he must
Keep an eye on aged beggars
Lest they strike him in disgust.

*

The Champion smiles – What Personality!
The Challenger scowls – How horrid he must be!
But let the Belt change hands and they change places –
Still from the same old corners come the same grimaces.

*

These public men who seem so to enjoy their dominion,
With their ruined faces and their voices treble with hate,
Are no less martyred because unaware of their fetters:
What would *you* be like were you never allowed to create
Or reflect, but compelled to give an immediate opinion,
Condemned to destroy or distribute the works of your
     betters?

*

          Hans-in-Kelder, Hans-in-Kelder,
               What are you waiting for?
          We need your strong arm to look after the farm
               And keep the wolf from the door.

          Hans-in-Kelder, Hans-in-Kelder,
               Came out of the parsley-bed,
          Came out at a run and levelled a gun
               And shot his old parents dead.

*

          With what conviction the young man spoke
          When he thought his nonsense rather a joke:
          Now, when he doesn't doubt any more,
          No one believes the booming old bore.

*

When statesmen gravely say – 'We must be realistic – '
The chances are they're weak and therefore pacifistic:
But when they speak of Principles – look out – perhaps
Their generals are already poring over maps.

*

– 'Don't you dream of a world, a society with no coercion?'
– 'Yes, where a foetus is able to refuse to be born.'

*

Only God can tell the saintly from the suburban,
Counterfeit virtues always resemble the true;
Neither in Life nor Art is honesty bohemian,
The free behave much as the respectable do.

*

To the man-in-the-street, who, I'm sorry to say,
      Is a keen observer of life,
The word Intellectual suggests straight away
      A man who's untrue to his wife.

*

What will cure the nation's ill?
A leader with a selfless will.
But how can you find this leader of yours?
By a process of Natural Selection of course.

The Way

Fresh addenda are published every day
To the encylopedia of the Way.

Linguistic notes and scientific explanations,
And texts for schools with modernized spelling and
    illustrations.

Now everyone knows the hero must choose the old
    horse,
Abstain from liquor and sexual intercourse

And look out for a stranded fish to be kind to:
Now everyone thinks he could find, had he a mind to,

The way through the waste to the chapel in the rock
For a vision of the Triple Rainbow or the Astral Clock.

Forgetting his information comes mostly from married
    men
Who liked fishing and a flutter on the horses now and
    then.

And how reliable can any truth be that is got
By observing oneself and then just inserting a Not?

Song for St Cecilia's Day

I

In a garden shady this holy lady
With reverent cadence and subtle psalm,
Like a black swan as death came on
Poured forth her song in perfect calm:
And by ocean's margin this innocent virgin
Constructed an organ to enlarge her prayer,
And notes tremendous from her great engine
Thundered out on the Roman air.

Blonde Aphrodite rose up excited,
Moved to delight by the melody,
White as an orchid she rode quite naked
In an oyster shell on top of the sea;
At sounds so entrancing the angels dancing
Came out of their trance into time again,
And around the wicked in Hell's abysses
The huge flame flickered and eased their pain.

Blessed Cecilia, appear in visions
To all musicians, appear and inspire:
Translated Daughter, come down and startle
Composing mortals with immortal fire.

II

I cannot grow;
I have no shadow
To run away from,
I only play.

I cannot err;
There is no creature
Whom I belong to,
Whom I could wrong.

I am defeat
When it knows it
Can now do nothing
By suffering.

All you lived through,
Dancing because you
No longer need it
For any deed.

I shall never be
Different. Love me.

O ear whose creatures cannot wish to fall,
O calm of spaces unafraid of weight,
Where Sorrow is herself, forgetting all
The gaucheness of her adolescent state,
Where Hope within the altogether strange
From every outworn image is released,
And Dread born whole and normal like a beast
Into a world of truths that never change:
Restore our fallen day; O re-arrange.

O dear white children casual as birds,
Playing among the ruined languages,
So small beside their large confusing words,
So gay against the greater silences
Of dreadful things you did: O hang the head,
Impetuous child with the tremendous brain,
O weep, child, weep, O weep away the stain,
Lost innocence who wished your lover dead,
Weep for the lives your wishes never led.

O cry created as the bow of sin
Is drawn across our trembling violin.
O weep, child, weep, O weep away the stain.
O law drummed out by hearts against the still
Long winter of our intellectual will.
That what has been may never be again.
O flute that throbs with the thanksgiving breath
Of convalescents on the shores of death.
O bless the freedom that you never chose.
O trumpets that unguarded children blow
About the fortress of their inner foe.
O wear your tribulation like a rose.

Many Happy Returns

(for John Rettger)

Johnny, since today is
February the twelfth when
Neighbours and relations
    Think of you and wish,
Though a staunch Aquarian,
Graciously accept the
Verbal celebrations
    Of a doubtful Fish.

Seven years ago you
Warmed your mother's heart by
Making a successful
    Début on our stage;
Naiveté's an act that
You already know you
Cannot get away with
    Even at your age.

So I wish you first a
Sense of theatre; only
Those who love illusion
    And know it will go far:
Otherwise we spend out
Lives in a confusion
Of what we say and do with
    Who we really are.

You will any day now
Have this revelation;
'Why, we're all like people
　　Acting in a play.'
And will suffer, Johnny,
Man's unique temptation
Precisely at the moment
　　You utter this cliché.

Remember if you can then,
Only the All-Father
Can change the cast or give them
　　Easier lines to say;
Deliberate interference
With others for their own good
Is not allowed the author
　　Of the play within The Play.

Just because our pride's an
Evil there's no end to,
Birthdays and the arts are
　　Justified, for when
We consciously pretend to
Own the earth or play at
Being gods, thereby we
　　Own that we are men.

As a human creature
You will all too often
Forget your proper station,
　　Johnny, like us all;
Therefore let your birthday
Be a wild occasion
Like a Saturnalia
　　Or a Servants' Ball.

What else shall I wish you?
Following convention
Shall I wish you Beauty
        Money, Happiness?
Or anything you mention?
No, for I recall an
Ancient proverb: – Nothing
        Fails like a success.

What limping devil sets our
Head and heart at variance,
That each time the Younger
        Generation sails,
The old and weather-beaten
Deny their own experience
And pray the gods to send them
        Calm seas, auspicious gales?

I'm not such an idiot
As to claim the power
To peer into the vistas
        Of your future, still
I'm prepared to guess you
Have not found your life as
Easy as your sister's
        And you never will.

If I'm right about this,
May you in your troubles,
Neither (like so many
        In the U.S.A.)
Be ashamed of any
Suffering as vulgar,
Nor bear them like a hero
        In the biggest way.

All the possibilities
It had to reject are
What give life and warmth to
        An actual character;
The roots of wit and charm tap
Secret springs of sorrow,
Every brilliant doctor
        Hides a murderer.

Then, since all self-knowledge
Tempts man into envy,
May you, by acquiring
        Proficiency in what
Whitehead calls the art of
Negative Prehension,
Love without desiring
        All that you are not.

Tao is a tightrope,
So to keep your balance,
May you always, Johnny,
        Manage to combine
Intellectual talents
With a sensual gusto,
The Socratic Doubt with
        The Socratic Sign.

That is all that I can
Think of at this moment
And it's time I brought these
        Verses to a close:
Happy Birthday, Johnny,
Live beyond your income,
Travel for enjoyment,
        Follow your own nose.

Shepherd's Carol

O lift your little pinkie
    And touch the winter sky:
Love is all over the mountains
    Where the beautiful go to die.

If Time were the wicked sheriff
    In a horse opera,
I'd pay for riding lessons
    And take his gun away.

If I were a Valentino
    And Fortune were a broad,
I'd hypnotise that iceberg
    Till she kissed me of her own accord.

If I'd stacked up the velvet
    And my crooked rib were dead,
I'd be breeding white canaries
    And eating crackers in bed.

But my cuffs are soiled and fraying
    The kitchen clock is slow,
And over the Blue Wonders
    The grass grew long ago.

I ain't speaking through the flowers
    Nor trying to explain,
But there ain't a living sorrow
    Comes wrapped in cellophane.

O solid is the sending
    Of the Boogie Woogie Man;
But who has found the horseshoes
    Or danced on Fiddler's Green?

O lift your little pinkie
  And touch the winter sky:
Love is all over the mountains
  Where the beautiful go to die.

Song of the Old Soldier

When the Sex War ended with the slaughter of the
        Grandmothers,
They found a bachelor's baby suffocating under them;
Somebody called him George and that was the end of it:
    They hitched him up to the Army.
    George, you old debutante,
    How did you get in the Army?

In the Retreat from Reason he deserted on his rocking-
        horse
And lived on a fairy's kindness till he tired of kicking
        her;
He smashed her spectacles and stole her cheque-book
        and mackintosh
    Then cruised his way back to the Army.
    George, you old numero,
    How did you get in the Army?

Before the Diet of Sugar he was using razor-blades
And exited soon after with an allergy to maidenheads;
He discovered a cure of his own, but no one would
        patent it,
    So he showed up again in the Army.
    George, you old flybynight,
    How did you get in the Army?

When the Vice Crusades were over he was hired by
        some Muscovites
Prospecting for deodorants among the Eskimos;

93

He was caught by a common cold and condemned to the
    whisky mines,
But schemozzled back to the Army.
George, you old Emperor,
How did you get in the Army?

Since Peace was signed with Honour he's been minding
    his business;
But, whoops, here comes His Idleness, buttoning his
    uniform;
Just in tidy time to massacre the Innocents;
He's come home to roost in the Army.
George, you old matador,
Welcome back to the Army.

Song of the Master and Boatswain

At Dirty Dick's and Sloppy Joe's
    We drank our liquor straight,
Some went upstairs with Margery,
    And some, alas, with Kate;
And two by two like cat and mouse
The homeless played at keeping house.

There Wealthy Meg, the Sailor's Friend,
    And Marion, cow-eyed,
Opened their arms to me but I
    Refused to step inside;
I was not looking for a cage
In which to mope in my old age.

The nightingales are sobbing in
    The orchards of our mothers,
And hearts that we broke long ago
  ˙ Have long been breaking others;
Tears are round, the sea is deep:
Roll them overboard and sleep.

Adrian and Francisco's Song

Adrian

The lovely lawns are swarming
    With people no one knows,
And up the marble staircase run
A hundred maladjusted girls
    In sensible black hose,
For milk and fifteen minutes fun
Between Creative Leatherwork and
    Hygiene of The Nose.

Francisco

Cupid no longer swishes,
    Venus no more behaves,
Committees take the earth in hand
To give the hills a thorough scrub
    And sterilize the waves;
The chef has died of horror, and
The war-horse and the battle-axe
    Have swept into their graves.

Chorus

    Well. Well. Well.
The Old World pooped at the party:
As the last waltz stopped, she whooped
    and flopped –
    'Small towns, my dear, are HELL.'
Lay her out in her black silk pyjamas,
    Let down your hair and cry:
Good little sunbeams must learn to fly,
But it's madly ungay when the goldfish die.
    Well. Well. Well.

Miranda's Song

My Dear One is mine as mirrors are lonely,
As the poor and sad are real to the good king,
And the high green hill sits always by the sea.

Up jumped the Black Man behind the elder tree,
Turned a somersault and ran away waving;
My Dear One is mine as mirrors are lonely.

The Witch gave a squawk; her venomous body
Melted into light as water leaves a spring
And the high green hill sits always by the sea.

At his crossroads, too, the Ancient prayed for me;
Down his wasted cheeks tears of joy were running:
My Dear One is mine as mirrors are lonely.

He kissed me awake, and no one was sorry;
The sun shone on sails, eyes, pebbles, anything,
And the high green hill sits always by the sea.

So, to remember our changing garden, we
Are linked as children in a circle dancing:
My Dear One is mine as mirrors are lonely,
And the high green hill sits always by the sea.

Three Songs from *The Age of Anxiety*

Deep in my dark the dream shines
Yes, of you, you dear always;
My cause to cry, cold but my
Story still, still my music.

Mild rose the moon, moving through our
Naked nights: tonight it rains;
Black umbrellas blossom out;
Gone the gold, my golden ball.

Heavy these hands. I believed
That pleased pause, your pause was me
To love alone till life's end:
I thought this; this was not true.

You touched, you took. Tears fall. O
Fair my far, when far ago
Like waterwheels wishes spun
Radiant robes: but the robes tore.

*

When Laura lay on her ledger side
And nicely threw her north cheek up,
How pleasing the plight of her promising grove
And how rich the random I reached with a rise.

*

Hushed is the lake of hawks
Bright with our excitement,
And all the sky of skulls
Glows with scarlet roses;
The melter of men and salt
Admires the drinker of iron:
Bold banners of meaning
Blaze o'er the host of days.

Under Which Lyre

A Reactionary Tract for the Times

(Phi Beta Kappa Poem, Harvard, 1946)

Ares at last has quit the field,
The bloodstains on the bushes yield
        To seeping showers,
And in their convalescent state
The fractured towns associate
        With summer flowers.

Encamped upon the college plain
Raw veterans already train
        As freshman forces;
Instructors with sarcastic tongue
Shepherd the battle-weary young
        Through basic courses.

Among bewildering appliances
For mastering the arts and sciences
        They stroll or run,
And nerves that never flinched at slaughter
Are shot to pieces by the shorter
        Poems of Donne.

Professors back from secret missions
Resume their proper eruditions,
        Though some regret it;
They liked their dictaphones a lot,
They met some big wheels, and do not
        Let you forget it.

But Zeus' inscrutable decree
Permits the will-to-disagree
    To be pandemic,
Ordains that vaudeville shall preach
And every commencement speech
    Be a polemic.

Let Ares doze, that other war
Is instantly declared once more
    'Twixt those who follow
Precocious Hermes all the way
And those who without qualms obey
    Pompous Apollo.

Brutal like all Olympic games,
Though fought with smiles and Christian names
    And less dramatic,
This dialectic strife between
The civil gods is just as mean,
    And more fanatic.

What high immortals do in mirth
Is life and death on Middle Earth;
    Their a-historic
Antipathy forever gripes
All ages and somatic types,
    The sophomoric

Who face the future's darkest hints
With giggles or with prairie squints
    As stout as Cortez,
And those who like myself turn pale
As we approach with ragged sail
    The fattening forties.

The sons of Hermes love to play,
And only do their best when they
      Are told they oughtn't;
Apollo's children never shrink
From boring jobs but have to think
      Their work important.

Related by antithesis,
A compromise between us is
      Impossible;
Respect perhaps but friendship never:
Falstaff the fool confronts forever
      The prig Prince Hal.

If he would leave the self alone,
Apollo's welcome to the throne,
      Fasces and falcons;
He loves to rule, has always done it;
The earth would soon, did Hermes run it,
      Be like the Balkans.

But jealous of our god of dreams,
His common-sense in secret schemes
      To rule the heart;
Unable to invent the lyre,
Creates with simulated fire
      Official art.

And when he occupies a college,
Truth is replaced by Useful Knowledge;
      He pays particular
Attention to Commercial Thought,
Public Relations, Hygiene, Sport,
      In his curricula.

Athletic, extrovert and crude,
For him, to work in solitude
      Is the offence,
The goal a populous Nirvana:
His shield bears this device: *Mens sana*
      Qui mal y pense.

Today his arms, we must confess,
From Right to Left have met success,
      His banners wave
From Yale to Princeton, and the news
From Broadway to the Book Reviews
      Is very grave.

His radio Homers all day long
In over-Whitmanated song
      That does not scan,
With adjectives laid end to end,
Extol the doughnut and commend
      The Common Man.

His, too, each homely lyric thing
On sport or spousal love or spring
      Or dogs or dusters,
Invented by some court-house bard
For recitation by the yard
      In filibusters.

To him ascend the prize orations
And sets of fugal variations
      On some folk-ballad,
While dietitians sacrifice
A glass of prune-juice or a nice
      Marsh-mallow salad.

Charged with his compound of sensational
Sex plus some undenominational
      Religious matter,
Enormous novels by co-eds
Rain down on our defenceless heads
      Till our teeth chatter.

In fake Hermetic uniforms
Behind our battle-line, in swarms
      That keep alighting,
His existentialists declare
That they are in complete despair,
      Yet go on writing.

No matter; He shall be defied;
White Aphrodite is on our side:
      What though his threat
To organize us grow more critical?
Zeus willing, we, the unpolitical,
      Shall beat him yet.

Lone scholars, sniping from the walls
Of learned periodicals,
      Our facts defend,
Our intellectual marines,
Landing in little magazines
      Capture a trend.

By night our student Underground
At cocktail parties whisper round
      From ear to ear;
Fat figures in the public eye
Collapse next morning, ambushed by
      Some witty sneer.

In our morale must lie our strength:
So, that we may behold at length
      Routed Apollo's
Battalions melt away like fog,
Keep well the Hermetic Decalogue,
      Which runs as follows: –

Thou shalt not do as the dean pleases,
Though shalt not write thy doctor's thesis
      On education,
Thou shalt not worship projects nor
Shalt thou or thine bow down before
      Administration.

Thou shalt not answer questionnaires
Or quizzes upon World-Affairs,
      Nor with compliance
Take any test. Thou shalt not sit
With statisticians nor commit
      A social science.

Thou shalt not be on friendly terms
With guys in advertising firms,
      Nor speak with such
As read the Bible for its prose,
Nor, above all, make love to those
      Who wash too much.

Thou shalt not live within thy means
Nor on plain water and raw greens.
      If thou must choose
Between the chances, choose the odd;
Read *The New Yorker*, trust in God;
      And take short views.

Nursery Rhyme

Their learned kings bent down to chat with frogs;
This was until the Battle of the Bogs.
The key that opens is the key that rusts.

Their cheerful kings made toffee on their stoves;
This was until the Rotting of the Loaves.
The robins vanish when the ravens come.

That was before the coaches reached the bogs;
Now woolly bears pursue the spotted dogs.
A witch can make an ogre out of mud.

That was before the weevils ate the loaves;
Now blinded bears invade the orange groves.
A witch can make an ogre out of mud.

The woolly bears have polished off the dogs;
Our bowls of milk are full of drowning frogs.
The robins vanish when the ravens come.

The blinded bears have rooted up the groves;
Our poisoned milk boils over on our stoves.
The key that opens is the key that rusts.

Barcarolle

(Aria from *The Rake's Progress*)

Gently, little boat,
Across the waters float,
Their crystal waves dividing;
 The sun in the west
 Is going to rest:
  Glide, glide, glide,
Towards the Islands of the Blest.

Orchards greenly grace
That undisturbèd place,
The wearied soul recalling
    To slumber and dream,
    While many a stream
        Falls, falls, falls,
Descanting on a child-like theme.

Lion, lamb and deer,
Untouched by greed or fear,
About its woods are straying,
    And quietly now
    The blossoming bough
        Sways, sways, sways
Above the clear unclouded brow.

Music Ho

The Emperor's favourite concubine
    Was in the Eunuch's pay,
The Wardens of the Marches turned
    Their spears the other way;
The vases crack, the ladies die,
    The Oracles are wrong:
We suck our thumbs or sleep; the show
    Is gamey and too long.

But – Music Ho! – at last it comes,
    The Transformation Scene:
A rather scruffy-looking god
    Descends in a machine
And, gabbling off his rustic rhymes,
    Misplacing one or two,
Commands the prisoners to walk,
    The enemies to screw.

The Love Feast

In an upper room at midnight
See us gathered on behalf
Of love according to the gospel
Of the radio-phonograph.

Lou is telling Anne what Molly
Said to Mark behind her back;
Jack likes Jill who worships George
Who has the hots for Jack.

Catechumens make their entrance;
Steep enthusiastic eyes
Flicker after tits and baskets;
Someone vomits; someone cries.

Willy cannot bear his father,
Lilian is afraid of kids;
The Love that rules the sun and stars
Permits what He forbids.

Adrian's pleasure-loving dachshund
In a sinner's lap lies curled;
Drunken absent-minded fingers
Pat a sinless world.

Who is Jenny lying to
By long-distance telephone?
The Love that made her out of nothing
Tells me to go home.

But that Miss Number in the corner
Playing hard to get . . .
I am sorry I'm not sorry . . .
Make me chaste, Lord, but not yet.

Song

Deftly, admiral, cast your fly
    Into the slow deep hover,
Till the wise old trout mistake and die;
    Salt are the deeps that cover
    The glittering fleets you led,
      White is your head.

Read on, ambassador, engrossed
    In your favourite Stendhal;
The Outer Provinces are lost,
    Unshaven horsemen swill
    The great wines of the Châteaux
      Where you danced long ago.

Do not turn, do not lift, your eyes
    Toward the still pair standing
On the bridge between your properties,
    Indifferent to your minding:
    In its glory, in its power,
      This is their hour.

Nothing your strength, your skill, could do
    Can alter their embrace
Or dispersuade the Furies who
    At the appointed place
    With claw and dreadful brow
      Wait for them now.

Limericks

A friend, who is not an ascetic,
Writes: 'Ireland, my dear, is *magnetic*.
   No snakes. Lots of elves
   Who just OFFER themselves –
Rather small but MOST sympathetic.'

*

A Young Person came out of the mists
Who had the most beautiful wrists:
   A scandal occurred
   Which has long been interred,
But the legend about them persists.

*

After vainly invoking the Muse,
A poet cried: 'Hell, what's the use?
   There's more inspiration
   At Grand Central Station;
I shall go there this moment and cruise.'

*

Said the Queen to the King: 'I don't frown on
The fact that you choose to go down on
   My page on the stairs
   But you'll give the boy airs
If you *will* do the job with your crown on.'

*

T. S. Eliot is quite at a loss
When clubwomen bustle across
    At literary teas,
    Crying: 'What, if you please,
Did you mean by *The Mill on the Floss*?'

*

The Bishop-Elect of Hong Kong
Has a cock which is ten inches long;
    He thinks the spectators
    Are admiring his gaiters
When he goes to the Gents – he is wrong.

*

To get the Last Poems of Yeats,
You need not mug up on dates;
    All a reader requires
    Is some knowledge of gyres
And the sort of people he hates.

*

There was a young poet whose sex
Was aroused by aesthetic effects;
    Marvell's *The Garden*
    Gave him a hard-on
And he came during *Oedipus Rex*.

Hunting Season

A shot: from crag to crag
    The tell-tale echoes trundle;
Some feathered he-or-she
    Is now a lifeless bundle
And, proud into a kitchen, some
Example of our tribe will come.

Down in the startled valley
    Two lovers break apart:
He hears the roaring oven
    Of a witch's heart;
Behind his murmurs of her name
She sees a marksman taking aim.

Reminded of the hour
    And that his chair is hard,
A deathless verse half done,
    One interrupted bard
Postpones his dying with a dish
Of several suffocated fish.

The Willow-Wren and the Stare

A starling and a willow-wren,
    On a may-tree by a weir,
Saw them meet and heard him say;
    'Dearest of my dear,
More lively than these waters chortling
    As they leap the dam,
My sweetest duck, my precious goose,
    My white lascivious lamb.'

With a smile she listened to him;
      Talking to her there:
What does he want? said the willow-wren;
      Much too much, said the stare.

'Forgive these loves who dwell in me,
      These brats of greed and fear,
The honking bottom-pinching clown,
      The snivelling sonneteer,
That so, between us, even these,
      Who till the grave are mine,
For all they fall so short of may,
      Dear heart, be still a sign.'
With a smile she closed her eyes,
      Silent she lay there:
Does he mean what he says? said the willow-wren;
      Some of it, said the stare.

'Hark! Wild Robin winds his horn
      And, as his notes require,
Now our laughter-loving spirits
      Must in awe retire
And let their kinder partners,
      Speechless with desire,
Go in their holy selfishness,
      Unfunny to the fire.'
Smiling, silently she threw
      Her arms about him there:
Is it only that? said the willow-wren;
      It's that as well, said the stare.

Waking in her arms he cried,
      Utterly content;
'I have heard the high good noises,
      Promoted for an instant,
Stood upon the shining outskirts
      Of that Joy I thank

For you, my dog and every goody.'
    There on the grass bank
She laughed, he laughed, they laughed together,
    Then they ate and drank:
Did he know what he meant? said the willow-wren
    God only knows, said the stare.

The Proof

'When rites and melodies begin
    To alter modes and times,
And timid bar-flies boast aloud
    Of uncommitted crimes,
And leading families are proud
    To dine with their black sheep,
What promises, what discipline,
    If any, will Love keep?'
        So roared Fire on their right:
            But Tamino and Pamina
            Walked past its rage,
        Sighing O, sighing O,
In timeless fermatas of awe and delight
    (Innocent? Yes. Ignorant? No.)
        Down the grim passage.

'When stinking Chaos lifts the latch,
    And Grotte backward spins,
And Helen's nose becomes a beak,
    And cats and dogs grow chins,
And daisies claw and pebbles shriek,
    And Form and Colour part,
What swarming hatreds then will hatch
    Out of Love's riven heart.'
        So hissed Water on their left:

But Pamina and Tamino
Opposed its spite,
With his worship, with her sweetness –
O look now! See how they emerge from the cleft
(Frightened? No. Happy? Yes.)
Out into sunlight.

'The Truest Poetry Is the Most Feigning'

(for Edgar Wind)

By all means sing of love but, if you do,
Please make a rare old proper hullabaloo:
When ladies ask *How much do you love me?*
The Christian answer is *così-così*.
But poets are not celibate divines;
Had Dante said so, who would read his lines?
Be subtle, various, ornamental, clever,
And do not listen to those critics ever
Whose crude provincial gullets crave in books
Plain cooking made still plainer by plain cooks,
As though the Muse preferred her half-wit sons;
Good poets have a weakness for bad puns.

Suppose your Beatrice be, as usual, late,
And you would tell us how it feels to wait,
You're free to think, what may be even true,
You're so in love that one hour seems like two,
But write – *As I sat waiting for her call,*
Each second longer darker seemed than all
(Something like this but more elaborate still)
Those raining centuries it took to fill
That quarry whence Endymion's love was torn;
From such ingenious fibs are poems born:
Then, should she leave you for some other guy,
Or ruin you with debts, or go and die,

No metaphor, remember, can express
A real historical unhappiness;
Your tears have value if they make us gay;
O Happy Grief! is all sad verse can say.

The living girl's your business (some odd sorts
Have been an inspiration to men's thoughts):
Yours may be old enough to be your mother,
Or have one leg that's shorter than the other,
Or play Lacrosse or do the Modern Dance;
To you that's destiny, to us it's chance;
We cannot love your love till she take on,
Through you, the wonders of a paragon.
Sing her triumphant passage to our land,
The sun her footstool, the moon in her right hand,
And seven planets blazing in her hair,
Queen of the Night and Empress of the Air;
Tell how her fleet by nine king swans is led,
Wild geese write magic letters overhead
And hippocampi follow in her wake
With Amphisbaene, gentle for her sake;
Sing her descent on the exulting shore
To bless the vines and put an end to war.

If half-way through such praises of your dear,
Riot and shooting fill the streets with fear,
And overnight, as in some terror dream,
Poets are suspect with the New Regime,
Stick at your desk and hold your panic in;
What you are writing may still save your skin:
Re-sex the pronouns, add a few details,
And, lo, a panegyric ode which hails
(How is the Censor, bless his heart, to know?)
The new pot-bellied Generalissimo.
Some epithets, of course, like *lily-breasted*
Need modifying to, say, *lion-chested*,
A title *Goddess of wry-necks and wrens*

To Great Reticulator of the fens,
But in an hour your poem qualifies
For a State pension or His annual prize,
And you will die in bed (which He will not:
That silly sausage will be hanged or shot).
Though honest Iagos, true to form, will write
Shame! in your margins, *Toady! Hypocrite!*,
True hearts, clear heads will hear the note of glory
And put inverted commas round the story,
Thinking – *Old Sly-boots! We shall never know
Her name or nature. Well, it's better so.*

For, given Man, by birth, by education,
Imago Dei who forgot his station,
The self-made creature who himself unmakes,
The only creature ever made who fakes,
With no more nature in his loving smile
Than in his theories of a natural style,
What but tall tales, the luck of verbal playing,
Can trick his lying nature into saying
That love, or truth in any serious sense,
Like orthodoxy, is a reticence.

Nocturne

Make this night loveable,
Moon, and with eye single
Looking down from up there,
Bless me, One especial
And friends everywhere.

With a cloudless brightness
Surround our absences;
Innocent be our sleeps,
Watched by great still spaces,
White hills, glittering deeps.

Parted by circumstance,
Grant each your indulgence
That we may meet in dreams
For talk, for dalliance,
By warm hearths, by cool streams.

Shine lest tonight any,
In the dark suddenly,
Wake alone in a bed
To hear his own fury
Wishing his love were dead.

Metalogue to *The Magic Flute*

(Lines composed in commemoration of the Mozart Bicentenary.
To be spoken by the singer playing the role of Sarastro)

Relax, Maestro, put your baton down:
Only the fogiest of the old will frown
If you the trials of the *Prince* prorogue
To let *Sarastro* speak this Metalogue,
A form acceptable to us, although
Unclassed by *Aristotle* or *Boileau*.
No modern audience finds it incorrect,
For interruption is what we expect
Since that new god, the Paid Announcer, rose,
Who with his quasi-Ossianic prose
Cuts in upon the lovers, halts the band,
To name a sponsor or to praise a brand.
Not that I have a product to describe
That you could wear or cook with or imbibe;
You cannot hoard or waste a work of art:
I come to praise but not to sell *Mozart*,
Who came into this world of war and woe
At Salzburg just two centuries ago,
When kings were many and machines were few,

And open Atheism something new.
(It makes a servantless New Yorker sore
To think sheer Genius had to stand before
A mere Archbishop with uncovered head:
But *Mozart* never had to make his bed.)

The history of Music as of Man
Will not go cancrizans, and no ear can
Recall what, when the Archduke *Francis* reigned,
Was heard by ears whose treasure-hoard contained
A *Flute* already but as yet no *Ring*:
Each age has its own mode of listening.
We know the *Mozart* of our fathers' time
Was gay, rococo, sweet, but not sublime,
A Viennese Italian; that is changed
Since music critics learned to feel 'estranged';
Now it's the Germans he is classed amongst,
A *Geist* whose music was composed from *Angst*,
At International Festivals enjoys
An equal status with the Twelve-Tone Boys;
He awes the lovely and the very rich,
And even those *Divertimenti* which
He wrote to play while bottles were uncorked,
Milord chewed noisily, Milady talked,
Are heard in solemn silence, score on knees,
Like quartets by the deafest of the *B*'s.
What next? One can no more imagine how,
In concert halls two hundred years from now,
When the Mozartian sound-waves move the air,
The cognoscenti will be moved, than dare
Predict how high orchestral pitch will go,
How many tones will constitute a row,
The tempo at which regimented feet
Will march about the Moon, the form of Suite
For Piano in a Post-Atomic Age,
Prepared by some contemporary *Cage*.

An opera composer may be vexed
By later umbrage taken at his text:
Even *Macaulay*'s schoolboy knows today
What *Robert Graves* or *Margaret Mead* would say
About the status of the sexes in this play,
Writ in that era of barbaric dark
'Twixt Modern Mom and Bronze-Age Matriarch.
Where now the Roman Fathers and their creed?
'Ah, where,' sighs *Mr Mitty*, 'Where indeed?'
And glances sideways at his vital spouse
Whose rigid jaw-line and contracted brows
Express her scorn and utter detestation
For Roman views of Female Education.
In Nineteen Fifty-Six we find the *Queen*
A highly-paid and most efficient Dean
(Who, as we all know, really runs the College),
Sarastro, tolerated for his knowledge,
Teaching the History of Ancient Myth
At *Bryn Mawr*, *Vassar*, *Bennington* or *Smith*;
Pamina may a *Time* researcher be
To let *Tamino* take his Ph.D.,
Acquiring manly wisdom as he wishes
While changing diapers and doing dishes;
Sweet *Papagena*, when she's time to spare,
Listens to *Mozart* operas on the air,
Though *Papageno*, one is sad to feel,
Prefers the juke box to the glockenspiel,
And how is – what was easy in the past –
A democratic villain to be cast?
Monostatos must make his bad impression
Without a race, religion or profession.

A work that lasts two hundred years is tough,
And operas, God knows, must stand enough:
What greatness made, small vanities abuse.
What must they not endure? The Diva whose
Fioriture and climactic note

118

The silly old composer never wrote,
Conductor *X*, that overrated bore
Who alters tempi and who cuts the score,
Director *Y* who with ingenious wit
Places his wretched singers in the pit
While dancers mime their roles, *Z* the Designer
Who sets the whole thing on an ocean liner,
The girls in shorts, the men in yachting caps;
Yet Genius triumphs over all mishaps,
Survives a greater obstacle than these,
Translation into foreign Operese
(English sopranos are condemned to *languish*
Because our tenors have to hide their *anguish*);
It soothes the *Frank*, it stimulates the *Greek*:
Genius surpasses all things, even Chic.
We who know nothing – which is just as well –
About the future, can, at least, foretell,
Whether they live in air-borne nylon cubes,
Practice group-marriage or are fed through tubes,
That crowds two centuries from now will press
(Absurd their hair, ridiculous their dress)
And pay in currencies, however weird,
To hear *Sarastro* booming through his beard,
Sharp connoisseurs approve if it is clean
The F in alt of the *Nocturnal Queen*,
Some uncouth creature from the *Bronx* amaze
Park Avenue by knowing all the *K*'s.

How seemly, then, to celebrate the birth
Of one who did no harm to our poor earth,
Created masterpieces by the dozen,
Indulged in toilet humour with his cousin
And had a pauper's funeral in the rain,
The like of whom we shall not see again:
How comely, also, to forgive; we should,
As *Mozart*, where he living, surely would,
Remember kindly *Salieri*'s shade,

Accused of murder and his works unplayed,
Nor, while we praise the dead, should we forget
We have *Stravinsky* – bless him – with us yet.
Basta! Maestro, make your minions play!
In all hearts, as in our finale, may
Reason & Love be crowned, assume their rightful sway.

A Toast

(Christ Church Gaudy, 1960)

What on earth does one say at a Gaudy,
　　On such an occasion as this,
O what, since I may not be bawdy,
　　Can I do except reminisce?
Middle-age with its glasses and dentures
　　(There's an opera about it by Strauss)
Puts an end to romantic adventures,
　　But not to my love of *The House*.

Ah! those Twenties before I was twenty,
　　When the news never gave one the glooms,
When the chef had minions in plenty,
　　And we could have lunch in our rooms.
In *Peck* there were marvellous parties
　　With bubbly and brandy and grouse,
And the aesthetes fought with the hearties:
　　It was fun, then, to be at *The House*.

National Service had not been suggested,
    O-Level and A were called Certs,
Our waistcoats were cut double-breasted,
    Our flannel trousers like skirts.
One could meet any day in Society
    Harold Acton, *Tom Driberg* or *Rowse*:
May there always, to lend their variety,
    Be some rather odd fish at *The House*.

The *Clarendon*'s gone – I regret her –
    The *George* is closed and forgot;
Some changes are all for the better,
    But *Woolworth*'s is probably not.
May the *Meadows* be only frequented
    By scholars and couples and cows:
God save us from all these demented
    Plans for a road through *The House*.

All those who wish well to our College
    Will wish her *Treasurer* well;
May Mammon give him foreknowledge
    Of just what to buy and to sell,
That all his investments on which her
    Income depends may be wows:
May She ever grow richer and richer,
    And the gravy abound at *The House*.

God bless and keep out of quarrels
    The *Dean*, the *Chapter* and *D*,
The *Censors* who shepherd our morals,
    Roy, *Hooky*, *Little* and me.
May those who come up next October
    Be *anständig*, have *esprit* and *nous*:
And now, though not overly sober,
    I give you a toast – TO THE HOUSE!

Some Thirty Inches from My Nose

Some thirty inches from my nose
The frontier of my Person goes,
And all the untilled air between
Is private *pagus* or demesne.
Stranger, unless with bedroom eyes
I beckon you to fraternize,
Beware of rudely crossing it:
I have no gun, but I can spit.

On the Circuit

Among pelagian travellers,
Lost on their lewd conceited way
To Massachusetts, Michigan,
Miami or L.A.,

An airborne instrument I sit,
Predestined nightly to fulfill
Columbia-Giesen-Management's
Unfathomable will,

By whose election justified,
I bring my gospel of the Muse
To fundamentalists, to nuns,
To Gentiles and to Jews,

And daily, seven days a week,
Before a local sense has jelled,
From talking-site to talking-site
Am jet-or-prop-propelled.

Though warm my welcome everywhere,
I shift so frequently, so fast,
I cannot now say where I was
The evening before last,

Unless some singular event
Should intervene to save the place,
A truly asinine remark,
A soul-bewitching face,

Or blessed encounter, full of joy,
Unscheduled on the Giesen Plan,
With, here, an addict of Tolkien,
There, a Charles Williams fan.

Since Merit but a dunghill is,
I mount the rostrum unafraid:
Indeed, 'twere damnable to ask
If I am overpaid.

Spirit is willing to repeat
Without a qualm the same old talk,
But Flesh is homesick for our snug
Apartment in New York.

A sulky fifty-six, he finds
A change of mealtime utter hell,
Grown far too crotchety to like
A luxury hotel.

The Bible is a goodly book
I always can peruse with zest,
But really cannot say the same
For Hilton's *Be My Guest*,

Nor bear with equanimity
The radio in students' cars,
Musak at breakfast, or – dear God! –
Girl-organists in bars.

Then, worst of all, the anxious thought,
Each time my plane begins to sink
And the No Smoking sign comes on:
What will there be to drink?

Is this a milieu where I must
How grahamgreeneish! How infra dig!
Snatch from the bottle in my bag
An analeptic swig?

Another morning comes: I see,
Dwindling below me on the plain,
The roofs of one more audience
I shall not see again.

God bless the lot of them, although
I don't remember which was which:
God bless the U.S.A., so large,
So friendly, and so rich.

Song of the Ogres

Little fellow, you're amusing,
Stop before you end by losing
    Your shirt:
Run along to Mother, Gus,
Those who interfere with us
    Get hurt.

Honest Virtue, old wives prattle,
Always wins the final battle.
    Dear, Dear!
Life's exactly what it looks,
Love may triumph in the books,
    Not here.

We're not joking, we assure you:
Those who rode this way before you
    Died hard.
What? Still spoiling for a fight?
Well, you've asked for it all right:
    On guard!

Always hopeful, aren't you? Don't be.
Night is falling and it won't be
  Long now:
You will never see the dawn,
You will wish you'd not been born.
  And how!

Song of the Devil

Ever since observation taught me temptation
Is a matter of timing, I've tried
To clothe my fiction in up-to-date diction,
The contemporary jargon of Pride.
    I can recall when, to win the more
        Obstinate round,
    The best bet was to say to them: 'Sin the more
        That Grace may abound.'

Since Social Psychology replaced Theology
The process goes twice as quick,
If a conscience is tender and loth to surrender
I have only to whisper: 'You're sick!'
    Puritanical morality
        Is madly Non-U:
    Enhance your personality
        With a Romance, with two.

'If you pass up a dame, you've yourself to blame,
For shame is neurotic, so snatch!
All rules are too formal, in fact they're abnormal,
For any desire is natch.
    So take your proper share, man, of
        Dope and drink:
    Aren't you the Chairman of
        Ego, Inc?

'Free-Will is a mystical myth as statistical
Methods have objectively shown,
A fad of the Churches: since the latest researches
Into Motivation it's known
    That Honour is hypocrisy,
        Honesty a joke.
    You live in a Democracy:
        Lie like other folk.

'Since men are like goods, what are shouldn'ts or shoulds
When you are the Leading Brand?
Let them all drop dead, you're way ahead,
Beat them up if they dare to demand
    What may your intention be,
        Or what might ensue:
    There's a difference of dimension be-
        tween the rest and you.

'If in the scrimmage of business your image
Should ever tarnish or stale,
Public Relations can take it and make it
Shine like a Knight of the Grail.
    You can mark up the price that you sell at, if
        Your package has glamour and show:
    Values are relative.
        Dough is dough.

'So let each while you may think you're more O.K.,
More yourself than anyone else,
Till you find that you're hooked, your goose is cooked,
And you're only a cypher of Hell's.
    Believe while you can that I'm proud of you,
        Enjoy your dream:
    I'm so bored with the whole fucking crowd of you
        I could *scream!*'

The Geography of the House

(for Christopher Isherwood)

Seated after breakfast
In this white-tiled cabin
Arabs call *The House where
Everybody goes*,
Even melancholics
Raise a cheer to Mrs
Nature for the primal
Pleasures She bestows.

Sex is but a dream to
Seventy-and-over,
But a joy proposed un-
-til we start to shave:
Mouth-delight depends on
Virtue in the cook, but
This She guarantees from
Cradle unto grave.

Lifted off the potty,
Infants from their mothers
Hear their first impartial
Words of worldly praise:
Hence, to start the morning
With a satisfactory
Dump is a good omen
All our adult days.

Revelation came to
Luther in a privy
(Cross-words have been solved there):
Rodin was no fool
When he cast his Thinker,
Cogitating deeply,
Crouched in the position
Of a man at stool.

All the Arts derive from
This ur-act of making,
Private to the artist:
Makers' lives are spent
Striving in their chosen
Medium to produce a
De-narcissus-ized en-
-during excrement.

Freud did not invent the
Constipated miser:
Banks have letter-boxes
Built in their façade
Marked *For Night Deposits*,
Stocks are firm or liquid,
Currencies of nations
Either soft or hard.

Global Mother, keep our
Bowels of compassion
Open through our lifetime,
Purge our minds as well:
Grant us a kind ending,
Not a second childhood,
Petulant, weak-sphinctered,
In a cheap hotel.

Keep us in our station:
When we get pound-noteish,
When we seem about to
Take up Higher Thought,
Send us some deflating
Image like the pained ex-
-pression on a Major
Prophet taken short.

(Orthodoxy ought to
Bless our modern plumbing:
Swift and St Augustine
Lived in centuries
When a stench of sewage
Ever in the nostrils
Made a strong debating
Point for Manichees.)

Mind and Body run on
Different time-tables:
Not until our morning
Visit here can we
Leave the dead concerns of
Yesterday behind us,
Face with all our courage
What is now to be.

Moralities

(Text after Aesop: Music by Hans Werner Henze)

I

Speaker

In the First Age the frogs dwelt
At peace in their pond: they paddled about,
Flies they caught and fat grew.

Courts they knew not, nor kings nor servants,
No laws they had, nor police nor jails:
All were equal, happy together.

The days went by in an unbroken calm:
Bored they grew, ungrateful for
Their good-luck, began to murmur.

Chorus

Higgledy-Piggledy,
What our Society
Needs is more Discipline,
Form and Degree.
Nobody wants to live
Anachronistically:
Lions have a Hierarchy,
Why shouldn't we?

Speaker

To mighty Jove on his jewelled throne
Went the Frog-Folk, the foolish people:
Thus they cried in chorus together.

Chorus

Hickory-Dockery,
Greatest Olympian,
Graciously grant the pe-
tition we bring.
Life as we know it is
Unsatisfactory,
We want a Monarchy,
Give us a King!

Foolish children, your choice is unwise.
But so be it: go back and wait.

Speaker

Into their pond from the heavens above,
With a splendid splash that sprayed them all,
Something fell, then floated around.

From the edge of their pond in awe they gazed,
The Frog-Folk, the foolish people:
Words they awaited, but no words came.

Chorus

He has no legs. He has no head.
Is he dumb? Is he deaf? Is he blind? Is he dead?
It's not a man. It's not a frog.
Why, it's nothing but a rotten old log!
Silly stump, watch me jump!
Tee-hee-hee, you can't catch me!
Boo to you! Boo! Boo! Boo!

Speaker

Back to Jove on his jewelled throne
Went the Frog-Folk, the foolish people:
Thus they cried in chorus together.

Chorus

    Jiggery-Pokery,
    Jove, you've insulted the
    Feelings of every
    Sensitive frog:
    What we demand is a
    Plenipotentiary

Sovereign, not an in-
animate log.

Bass Solo

By the hard way must the unwise learn.
So be it: go back and wait.

Speaker

On their pond from the heavens above,
Cruel-beaked, a crane alighted.
Fierce, ravenous, a frog-eater.

Doom was upon them, Dread seized
The Frog-Folk, the foolish people:
They tried to escape. It was too late.

Chorus

No! No! Woe! Woe! O! O! O . . .

Speaker

If people are too dumb to know when all is well with them,
The gods shrug their shoulders and say: – To Hell with
them.

II

Speaker

When first had no second, before Time was,
Mistress Kind, the Mother of all things,
Summoned the crows: they crowded before Her.

Alto Solo

Dun must you be, not dainty to behold,
For your gain, though, I grace you with the gift of song:

132

Well shall you warble, as welcome to the ear
As the lively lark or loud nightingale.
Go in peace.

Speaker

      Gaily they went,
And daily at dawn with dulcet voices
Tooted in the tree-tops a tuneful madrigal.

Chorus

Now, glorious in the East, the day is breaking:
Creatures of field and forest, from your sleep awaking,
Consort your voices, fearless of exposure,
And of yourselves now make a free disclosure,
Your pitch of presence to the world proclaiming,
Expressing, affirming, uttering and naming,
And each in each full recognition finding
No scornful echo but a warm responding,
Your several notes not harsh nor interfering,
But all in joy and concord co-inhering.

Speaker

So they chanted till by chance one day
Came within earshot where the crows were nesting
A stand of horses, stallions and mares,
Whinneying and neighing as their wont in Spring is.

Chorus

How strange! How astonishing! What astonishing
    sounds!
Never have we heard such noises as these.
It's so . . . so . . . so . . . so . . . so IT!
How new, How new! We must be too. What a break-
    through!

Away with dominant and tonic!
Let's be chic and electronic.
Down with the Establishment!
Up with non-music, the Sound-Event!
Arias are out and neighing is in:
Hurrah for horses! Let us begin.

Speaker

But crows are no more horses than chutney is tabasco:
Their efforts at *aggiornomento* ended in fiasco.

Chorus

CAW! CAW! CAW! CAW! CAW!

III

Speaker

A ship put to sea, sailed out of harbour
On a peaceful morning with passengers aboard.
The sun was shining, but the ship's Captain,
Weather-wise, watching the sky,
Warned his crew.

Bass Solo

Wild will be tonight
With a gurling gale and great waves.
To your storm stations! Stand by!

Chorus

O Captain, Captain, tell us the truth!
Are we doomed to drown in the deep sea?

While my body breathes I will battle for our lives,
But our fate lies now in Neptune's hands.

Ah! What shall we do? The ship is about to founder,
Overwhelmed by the waves that so wildly surround her.
Neptune at our sins is righteously offended:
Over the deck his dreadful trident is extended.

Neptune, Neptune, forgive us! We confess it sadly,
We have neglected Thy worship and acted very badly.
Forgive us! Have mercy, have mercy, and be our Saviour,
And for ever after we will alter our behaviour.

Neptune, thou Strong One, stop this outrageous welter,
Restrain the wind and waft us safely into shelter:
Bulls we will bring to Thine altar and incense offer,
With treasures of great price fill up Thy temple coffer.

The wind is falling, the waves are less,
The clouds scatter, the sky lightens:
By the kindness of Neptune we have come through.

We knew He was joking, not serious:
Who would harm nice people like us?

In this merry month of May,
        Dew on leaves a-sparkle,
Of youth and love and laughter sing,
        Dancing in a circle.

Over hill, over dale,
    Over the wide water,
Jack McGrew is come to woo
    Jill, the oil-king's daughter.

Come from afar in his motor-car,
    Eager to show devotion,
Looking so cute in his Sunday Suit,
    And smelling of shaving-lotion.

Here comes the Bride at her Father's side,
    Fresh as thyme or parsley:
Blushing now, to the Bridegroom's bow
    She answers with a curtsey.

Boys Semi-Chorus

Kiss her once, kiss her twice,
    Bring her orchids on a salver,
Spit in her eye if she starts to cry,
    And send her to Charlie Colver.

Girls Semi-Chorus

Feed the brute with eggs and fruit,
    Keep him clean and tidy,
Give him what-for if he starts to snore,
    And scold him every Friday.

Chorus

We wish you health, we wish you wealth,
    And seven smiling children,
Silver-bright be every night,
    And every day be golden.

Captain, why do you sit apart,
Frowning over your nautical chart?
Blue is the sky and bright is the sun:
Leave your bridge and join the fun.

Bass Solo

The sky is blue, the sun is bright,
But who laughs in the morning may weep before night.

Chorus

Your gloom does not enlighten us:
We will not let you frighten us.

An acid-drop for the Corner Cop,
    A crab-apple for Teacher,
Some mouldy fudge for His Honour the Judge,
    And a Bronx Cheer for the Preacher.

Speaker

When afraid, men pray to the gods in all sincerity,
But worship only themselves in their days of prosperity.

A New Year Greeting

(After an Article by Mary J. Marples in *Scientific American*,
January 1969)
(for Vassily Yanowsky)

On this day tradition allots
    to taking stock of our lives,
my greetings to all of you, Yeasts,
    Bacteria, Viruses,

Aerobics and Anaerobics:
        A Very Happy New Year
to all for whom my ectoderm
        is as Middle-Earth to me.

For creatures your size I offer
        a free choice of habitat,
so settle yourselves in the zone
        that suits you best, in the pools
of my pores or the tropical
        forests of arm-pit and crotch,
in the deserts of my fore-arms,
        or the cool woods of my scalp.

Build colonies: I will supply
        adequate warmth and moisture,
the sebum and lipids you need,
        on condition you never
do me annoy with your presence,
        but behave as good guests should,
not rioting into acne
        or athlete's-foot or a boil.

Does my inner weather affect
        the surfaces where you live?
Do unpredictable changes
        record my rocketing plunge
from fairs when the mind is in tift
        and relevant thoughts occur
to fouls when nothing will happen
        and no one calls and it rains.

I should like to think that I make
        a not impossible world,
but an Eden it cannot be:
        my games, my purposive acts,

may turn to catastrophes there.
        If you were religious folk,
how would your dramas justify
        unmerited suffering?

By what myths would your priests account
        for the hurricanes that come
twice every twenty-four hours,
        each time I dress or undress,
when, clinging to keratin rafts,
        whole cities are swept away
to perish in space, or the Flood
        that scalds to death when I bathe?

Then, sooner or later, will dawn
        a day of Apocalypse,
when my mantle suddenly turns
        too cold, too rancid, for you,
appetizing to predators
        of a fiercer sort, and I
am stripped of excuse and nimbus,
        a Past, subject to Judgement.

Doggerel by a Senior Citizen

(for Robert Lederer)

Our earth in 1969
Is not the planet I call mine,
The world, I mean, that gives me strength
To hold off chaos at arm's length.

My Eden landscapes and their climes
Are constructs from Edwardian times,
When bath-rooms took up lots of space,
And, before eating, one said Grace.

The automobile, the aeroplane,
Are useful gadgets, but profane:
The enginry of which I dream
Is moved by water or by steam.

Reason requires that I approve
The light-bulb which I cannot love:
To me more reverence-commanding
A fish-tail burner on the landing.

My family ghosts I fought and routed,
Their values, though, I never doubted:
I thought their Protestant Work-Ethic
Both practical and sympathetic.

When couples played or sang duets,
It was immoral to have debts:
I shall continue till I die
To pay in cash for what I buy.

The Book of Common Prayer we knew
Was that of 1662:
Though with-it sermons may be well,
Liturgical reforms are hell.

Sex was, of course – it always is –
The most enticing of mysteries,
But news-stands did not yet supply
Manichaean pornography.

Then Speech was mannerly, an Art,
Like learning not to belch or fart:
I cannot settle which is worse,
The Anti-Novel or Free Verse.

Nor are those Ph.D.'s my kith,
Who dig the symbol and the myth:
I count myself a man of letters
Who writes, or hopes to, for his betters.

Dare any call Permissiveness
An educational success?
Saner those class-rooms which I sat in,
Compelled to study Greek and Latin.

Though I suspect the term is crap,
If there *is* a Generation Gap,
Who is to blame? Those, old or young,
Who will not learn their Mother-Tongue.

But Love, at least, is not a state
Either *en vogue* or out-of-date,
And I've true friends, I will allow,
To talk and eat with here and now.

Me alienated? Bosh! It's just
As a sworn citizen who must
Skirmish with it that I feel
Most at home with what is Real.

Except for previously unpublished or uncollected poems, the texts in this book are based on the early printed editions, with corrections from manuscripts and other sources. The texts do not reflect the cuts and changes Auden made for his later collected editions. Where a poem had no title in the early editions, the title used here is either the first line or a title that Auden added in later collections; some titles, noted here, have been supplied by the editor for this volume. Poems that Auden left unpublished, or that he printed in magazine but did not collect in book form, are noted here.

Page

3 *It's No Use Raising a Shout.* Written November 1929.

4 *What's in Your Mind, My Dove, My Coney.* Written November 1930.

4 *Prothalamion.* Written in Summer 1930 as a chorus for Auden's lost play *The Fronny*; used again in 1935 as a chorus in Auden and Christopher Isherwood's play *The Dog Beneath the Skin*.

6 *Alma Mater.* Originally written in 1930 as a chorus for a night-club scene in *The Fronny* and used again in 1933 as a chorus in Auden's play *The Dance of Death*; title supplied for this edition. Not published separately by Auden.

8 *The Airman's Alphabet.* Written as a separate poem in June 1931 and shortly afterward incorporated into the 'Journal of an Airman' in *The Orators*; not published separately by Auden.

11 *The Three Companions.* Written October 1931; originally the epilogue to *The Orators*.

11 *Shorts.* Written 1929–31; title supplied for this edition. Mostly unpublished during Auden's lifetime; some are printed here for the first time. 'Let us honour if we can' was the dedicatory poem to Christopher Isherwood in Auden's first published volume, 1930 *Poems*. 'Private faces in public places' was the dedicatory poem to Stephen Spender in *The Orators*. Auden and Isherwood used 'If yer wants to see me agyne' and 'Alice is gone and I'm alone' (without the final stanza) as songs in *The Dog Beneath the Skin*.

15 *Song: 'You were a great Cunarder, I'.* Written probably in 1932 and used as a song in *The Dance of Death*; not published separately by Auden.

15 *Ballad: 'O what is that sound which so thrills the ear'.* Written October 1932.

17 *The Witnesses.* This is the complete version of this poem,

written late in 1932 and, after appearing in the *Listener*, 12 July 1933, never reprinted or collected by Auden; he revised the third part as a chorus for *The Dog Beneath the Skin* and as a separate poem in later collections.

22 *Song: 'Seen when night was silent'*. Probably written in 1933; used as a song in *The Dog Beneath the Skin*.

23 *Who's Who*. Probably written in 1934, after Auden reviewed a biography of Lawrence of Arabia.

23 *Now Through Night's Caressing Grip*. Written in 1935 as a chorus for *The Dog Beneath the Skin*.

24 *In the Square*. Written Spring 1935; the title is from the poem's first appearance in the *Spectator*, 31 May 1935.

25 *Madrigal*. Written June 1935 as a chorus, set by Benjamin Britten, for the documentary film *Coal Face*, made by the General Post Office Film Unit.

26 *Night Mail*. Written in July 1935 as a spoken commentary to the last part of the documentary film of the same name.

28 *Song: 'Let the florid music praise'*. Written February 1936.

28 *Foxtrot from a Play*. Written March 1936; a few lines were used almost immediately as a song in Auden and Isherwood's play *The Ascent of F6*. The full text appeared under this title in *New Verse*, April–May 1936, but it was never collected by Auden.

30 *Underneath the Abject Willow*. Written March 1936.

31 *Fish in the Unruffled Lakes*. Written March 1936.

32 *Song: 'The chimney sweepers'*. Written probably in March 1936 for *The Ascent of F6*, but not published separately by Auden; title supplied for this edition.

32 *At Last the Secret is Out*. Written probably in April 1936 as a chorus for *The Ascent of F6*.

33 *Funeral Blues*. First written April 1936 for *The Ascent of F6*; rewritten in June 1937 as a cabaret song to be sung by Hedli Anderson. The version in *The Ascent of F6* was a dirge sung after the mountaineer hero dreams that his brother, a high colonial official, has suddenly died. In the play, the first two stanzas were the same as those in the rewritten version, but they were followed by these three stanzas, which refer to other characters who accompany the hero on his climb:

> Hold up your umbrellas to keep off the rain
> From Doctor Williams while he opens a vein;
> Life, he pronounces, it is finally extinct.
> Sergeant, arrest that man who said he winked!
>
> Shawcross will say a few words sad and kind
> To the weeping crowds about the Master-Mind,

While Lamp with a powerful microscope
Searches their faces for a sign of hope.

And Gunn, of course, will drive the motor-hearse:
None could drive it better, most would drive it worse.
He'll open up the throttle to its fullest power
And drive him to the grave at ninety miles an hour.

34 *Jam Tart*. Written probably around April 1936 as a cabaret song
to be set by Benjamin Britten and sung by Hedli Anderson;
the title may have been chosen by Britten. First published
posthumously in 'Uncollected Songs and Lighter Poems,
1936–40', ed. by Nicholas Jenkins, *Auden Studies 2* (1994).

35 *Death's Echo*. Written September 1936.

37 *Lullaby: 'Lay your sleeping head, my love'*. Written January 1937.

38 *Danse Macabre*. Written January 1937.

41 *Blues: 'Ladies and gentlemen, sitting here'*. Written probably early
in 1937; printed in *New Verse*, May 1937, but never collected by
Auden.

42 *Give Up Love*. Written probably around April 1937 as a cabaret
song to be set by Benjamin Britten and sung by Hedli
Anderson; title supplied for this edition. First published
posthumously in 'Uncollected Songs and Lighter Poems,
1936–40', ed. by Nicholas Jenkins, *Auden Studies 2* (1994).

44 *Nonsense Song*. Written probably in Spring 1937, perhaps for an
anthology of children's poetry that was never published; title
supplied for this edition. First published posthumously in
'Uncollected Songs and Lighter Poems, 1936–40', ed. by
Nicholas Jenkins, *Auden Studies 2* (1994).

44 *Johnny*. Written April 1937.

45 *Miss Gee*. Written April 1937.

49 *Victor*. Written June 1937.

53 *James Honeyman*. Written August 1937.

58 *Roman Wall Blues*. Written October 1937 for the radio script
Hadrian's Wall.

59 *As I Walked Out One Evening*. Written November 1937.

61 *O Tell Me the Truth About Love*. Written January 1938.

63 *Gare du Midi*. Written in Brussels, December 1938.

63 *Epitaph on a Tyrant*. Written January 1939.

64 *The Unknown Citizen*. Written March 1939.

65 *Refugee Blues*. Written March 1939.

67 *Ode*. Written probably in March 1939; not published in
Auden's lifetime. Auden inscribed the poem to the manager
and staff of the hotel where he stayed during his first weeks in
New York. S.A. = sex appeal.

68 *Calypso*. Written May 1939.

69 *Heavy Date*. Written October 1939.

74 *Song: Warm are the Still and Lucky Miles*. Written October 1939.

75 *'Gold in the North' Came the Blizzard to Say*. Written probably around November 1939 for the libretto of the operetta *Paul Bunyan*.

76 *The Glamour Boys and Girls Have Grievances Too*. Written probably around November 1939 for *Paul Bunyan*; published under this title in *The New Yorker*, 24 August 1940, but never collected by Auden.

78 *Carry Her Over the Water*. Written probably in December 1939 for *Paul Bunyan*.

78 *Eyes Look into the Well*. Written probably in April 1940 for the radio play *The Dark Valley*.

79 *Lady Weeping at the Crossroads*. Written probably in April 1940 for *The Dark Valley*.

80 *Notes*. Written in Summer 1940 for the 'Notes' to the long poem 'New Year Letter'.

85 *The Way*. Written in Summer 1940 as part of the sonnet sequence 'The Quest'.

85 *Song for St Cecilia's Day*. Written July 1940.

88 *Many Happy Returns*. Written February 1942.

92 *Shepherd's Carol*. Written in Spring 1942 for the long poem 'For the Time Being: A Christmas Oratorio', but dropped before publication. Partly set by Benjamin Britten, who devised the title and published his setting. The full text is printed here for the first time.

93 *Song of the Old Soldier*. Written in Spring 1942 for 'For the Time Being'.

94 *Song of the Master and Boatswain*. Written around December 1942 for 'The Sea and the Mirror: A Commentary on Shakespeare's *The Tempest*'.

95 *Adrian and Francisco's Song*. Written around January 1943 for 'The Sea and the Mirror'. This early draft version is printed here for the first time; the version published in 'The Sea and the Mirror' consists only of the third and second lines from the end.

96 *Miranda's Song*. Written around January 1943 for 'The Sea and the Mirror'.

96 *Three Songs from* The Age of Anxiety. Written probably in 1945 and 1946. In the prose narration in *The Age of Anxiety* the first of these is described as a jukebox song titled 'The Case is Closed' and the second is 'a verse from an old prospector's ballad' (most of the suggestive terms have a technical use in

mining). In the third song the four elements are identified indirectly: the 'lake of hawks' is air; 'sky of skulls' is earth; 'melter of men and salt' is fire; 'drinker of iron' is water.

98 *Under Which Lyre*. Written in Spring 1946 for the annual Phi Beta Kappa ceremony at Harvard University.

104 *Nursery Rhyme*. Written January 1947.

104 *Barcarolle*. Written around February 1948 for the libretto for *The Rake's Progress*; Auden collected the poem under this title in *The Shield of Achilles*.

105 *Music Ho*. Written May 1948.

106 *The Love Feast*. Written May 1948.

107 *Song: Deftly, admiral, cast your fly*. Written June 1948.

108 *Limericks*. Written in Autumn 1950. Auden published three: 'A Young Person', 'T. S. Eliot' and 'To get the Last Poems'. The rest are here printed or collected for the first time, in texts found in Auden's letters to friends or, in the case of 'Said the Queen to the King', transcribed from memory by Auden's friend Alan Ansen.

110 *Hunting Season*. Written 1952.

110 *The Willow-Wren and the Stare*. Written 1953.

112 *The Proof*. Written August 1953.

113 *'The Truest Poetry is the Most Feigning'*. Written around September 1953.

115 *Nocturne*. Written October 1953.

116 *Metalogue to* The Magic Flute. Written 1955.

120 *A Toast*. Probably written 1958, although not read at Christ Church until 1960.

122 *Some Thirty Inches from My Nose*. Written around 1962.

122 *On the Circuit*. Written around June 1963.

124 *Song of the Ogres*. Written around December 1963 as one of the lyrics Auden was commissioned to write for the musical play *Man of La Mancha* before the producer turned to another lyricist.

125 *Song of the Devil*. Written around December 1963 for *Man of La Mancha*.

127 *The Geography of the House*. Written July 1964.

129 *Moralities*. Written 1967.

137 *A New Year Greeting*. Written May 1969.

139 *Doggerel by a Senior Citizen*. Written May 1969.

A friend, who is not an ascetic, 108
A nondescript express, in from the South, 63
A shilling life will give you all the facts, 23
A shot: from crag to crag, 110
A starling and a willow-wren, 110
A Young Person came out of the mists, 108
ACE – Pride of parents, 8
Adrian and Francisco's Song, 95
After vainly invoking the Muse, 108
Airman's Alphabet, The, 8
Alice is gone and I'm alone, 14
Alma Mater, 6
Among pelagian travelers, 122
Ares at last has quit the field, 98
As I walked out one evening, 59
At Dirty Dick's and Sloppy Joe's, 94
At last the secret is out, as it always must come in the end, 32

Ballad: O What is that sound which so thrills the ear, 15
Barcarolle, 104
Base words are uttered only by the base, 82
Blues, 41
By all means sing of love but, if you do, 113

Calypso, 68
Carry her over the water, 78
Cleopatra, Anthony, 42
Come kiss me now, you old brown cow, 14

Danse Macabre, 38
Death's Echo, 35
Deep in my dark the dream shines, 96
Deftly, admiral, cast your fly, 107
Desire for death in the morning, 12
Do we want to return to the womb? Not at all, 82
Doggerel by a Senior Citizen, 139
Don't know my father's name, 14
'Don't you dream of a world, a society with no coercion?', 84
Driver drive faster and make a good run, 68

Epitaph on a Tyrant, 63
Ever since observation taught me temptation, 125
Eyes look into the well, 78

Fish in the unruffled lakes, 31
Foxtrot from a Play, 28
Fresh addenda are published every day, 85
Funeral Blues, 33

Gare du Midi, 63
Gently, little boat, 104
Geography of the House, The, 127
Give Up Love, 42
Glamour Boys and Girls Have Grievances Too, The, 76
'Gold in the North' came the blizzard to say, 75

Hail the strange electric writing, 6
Hans-in-Kelder, Hans-in-Kelder, 83
He was found by the Bureau of Statistics to be, 64
Heavy Date, 69
His ageing nature is the same, 81
Hunting Season, 110
Hushed is the lake of hawks, 97

I am beginning to lose patience, 13
I'm afraid there's many a spectacled sod, 13
I'm a jam tart, I'm a bargain basement, 34
If yer wants to see me agyne, 14
In a garden shady this holy lady, 85
In an upper room at midnight, 106
In the First Age the frogs dwelt, 129
In the Square, 24
In this epoch of high-pressure selling, 67
Infants in their mothers' arms, 81
It's farewell to the drawing-room's civilized cry, 38
It's no use raising a shout, 3

Jam Tart, 34
James Honeyman, 53
James Honeyman was a silent child, 53
Johnny, 44
Johnny, since today is, 88

Ladies and gentlemen, sitting here, 41
Lady, weeping at the crossroads, 79
Lay your sleeping head, my love, 37
Let me tell you a little story, 45
Let the florid music praise, 28
Let us honour if we can, 13
Limericks, 108
Little fellow, you're amusing, 124
Love Feast, The, 106
Lullaby, 37

Madrigal, 25
Make this night loveable, 115
Man would be happy, loving and sage, 12
Many Happy Returns, 88
Metalogue to The Magic Flute, 116
Miranda's Song, 96
Miss Gee, 45
Moralities, 129
Music Ho, 105
My Dear One is mine as mirrors are lonely, 96
My love is like a red red rose, 44

New Year Greeting, A, 137
Night Mail, 26
Nocturne, 115
Nonsense Song, 44
Notes, 80
Now through night's caressing grip, 23
Nursery Rhyme, 104

O for doors to be open and an invite with gilded edges, 24
O lift your little pinkie, 92
O lurcher-loving collier, black as night, 25
O Tell Me the Truth About Love, 61
O the valley in the summer where I and my John, 44
O what is that sound which so thrills the ear, 15
'O where are you going' said reader to rider, 11
'O who can ever gaze his fill,' 35
Ode: In this epoch of high-pressure selling, 67
On the Circuit, 122
On this day tradition allots, 137
Once for candy cook had stolen, 82
Only God can tell the saintly from the suburban, 84

Our earth in 1969, 139
Over the heather the wet wind blows, 58

Parents once upon a time, 80
Perfection, of a kind, was what he was after, 63
Pick a quarrel, go to war, 11
Private faces in public places, 14
Proof, The, 112
Prothalamion, 4

Refugee Blues, 65
Relax, Maestro, put your baton down, 116
Roman Wall Blues, 58

Said the Queen to the King: 'I don't frown on', 108
Say this city has ten million souls, 65
Schoolboy, making lonely maps, 13
Seated after breakfast, 127
Seen when night was silent, 22
Sharp and silent in the, 69
Shepherd's Carol, 92
Shorts, 11
Some say that Love's a little boy, 61
Some thirty inches from my nose, 122
Song: Deftly, admiral, cast your fly, 107
Song: Let the florid music praise, 28
Song: Seen when night was silent, 22
Song: The chimney sweepers, 32
Song: Warm are the still and lucky miles, 74
Song: You were a great Cunarder, 15
Song for St Cecilia's Day, 85
Song of the Devil, 125
Song of the Master and Boatswain, 94
Song of the Ogres, 124
Song of the Old Soldier, 93
Stop all the clocks, cut off the telephone, 33

T. S. Eliot is quite at a loss, 109
The Bishop-Elect of Hong Kong, 109
The Champion smiles – What Personality!, 83
The chimney sweepers, 32
The Emperor's favourite concubine, 105
The friends of the born nurse, 11
The lovely lawns are swarming, 95
The pleasures of the English nation, 13

The soldier loves his rifle, 28
'The Truest Poetry Is the Most Feigning', 113
Their learned kings bent down to chat with frogs, 104
There are two kinds of friendship even in babes, 13
There was a young poet whose sex, 109
These public men who seem so to enjoy their dominion, 83
This is the Night Mail crossing the Border, 26
Three Companions, The, 11
Three Songs from The Age of Anxiety, 96
To get the Last Poems of Yeats, 109
To the man-in-the-street, who, I'm sorry to say, 84
Toast, A, 120
Tommy did as mother told him, 12

Under Which Lyre, 98
Underneath the abject willow, 30
Unkown Citizen, The, 64

Victor, 49
Victor was a little baby, 49

Warm are the still and lucky miles, 74
Way, The, 85
What on earth does one say at a Gaudy, 120
What will cure the nation's ill?, 84
What's in your mind, my dove, my coney, 4
When Laura lay on her ledger side, 97
'When rites and melodies begin', 112
When statesmen gravely say – 'We must be realistic – ', 84
When the Sex War ended with the slaughter of the
    Grandmothers, 93
Who's Who, 23
Willow-Wren and the Stare, The, 110
Willy, finding half a soul, 12
With what conviction the young man spoke, 83
Witnesses, The, 17

You dowagers with Roman noses, 17
You were a great Cunarder, 15
You who return tonight to a narrow bed, 4
You're a long way off from becoming a saint, 12
You've no idea how dull it is, 76